THE WORKING LIFE

A Roman Senator

THE WORKING LIFE

A Roman Senator

THE WORKING LIFE

A Roman Senator

DON NARDO

LUCENT
BOOKS ®

THOMSON

★

™

GALE

San Diego • Detroit • New York • San Francisco • Cleveland • New Haven, Conn. • Waterville, Maine • London • Munich

For more information, contact
Lucent Books
27500 Drake Rd.
Farmington Hills, MI 48331-3535
Or you can visit our Internet site at http://www.gale.com

LIBRARY OF CONGRESS CATALOGING-IN-PUBLICATION DATA

Nardo, Don, 1947–
    A Roman senator / by Don Nardo.
        p. cm. — (The working life series).
Includes bibliographical references and index
    ISBN 1-59018-481-5 (hardcover : alk. pape.)
    1. Rome—History—Republic, 510–30 B.C.—Juvenile literature. 2. Rome—Senate—Juvenile literature. 3. Nobility—Rome—Juvenile literature. I. Title. II. Series.
    DG235.2.N37 2004
    328'.0937'6—dc22
                                                                    2004010691

Printed in the United States of America

CONTENTS

FOREWORD

"The strongest bond of human sympathy outside the family relations should be one uniting all working people of all nations and tongues and kindreds."

Abraham Lincoln, 1864

Work is a common activity in which almost all people engage. It is probably the most universal of human experiences. As Henry Ford, inventor of the Model T said, "There will never be a system invented which will do away with the necessity of work." For many people, work takes up most of their day. They spend more time with their coworkers than with family and friends. And the common goals people pursue on the job may be among the first thoughts that they have in the morning, and the last that they may have at night.

While the idea of work is universal, the way it is done and who performs it vary considerably throughout history. The story of work is inextricably tied to the history of technology, the history of culture, and the history of gender and race. When the typewriter was invented, for example, it was considered the exclusive domain of men who worked as secretaries. As women workers became more accepted, the secretarial role was gradually filled by women. Finally, with the invention of the computer, the modern secretary spends little time actually typing correspondence. Files are delivered via computer, and more time is spent on other tasks than the manual typing of correspondence and business.

This is just one example of how work brings together technology, gender, and culture. Another example is the American plantation slave. The harvesting of cotton was initially so cumbersome and time consuming that even with slaves its profitability was doubtful. With the invention of the cotton gin, however, efficiency improved, and slavery became a viable agricultural tool. It also became a southern tradition and institution, enough that the South was willing to go to war to preserve it.

The books in Lucent's Working Life series strive to show the intermingling of work, and its reflection in culture, technology, race, and gender. Indeed, history viewed through the perspective of the average worker is both enlightening and fascinating. Take the history of the typewriter, mentioned above. Readers today have access to more technology than any of their historical counterparts, and, in fact, though they would find the typewriter's keyboard familiar, they would find using it a bore. Finding out that people spent their days sitting over that machine (with no talk of carpal tunnel syndrome!) and were valued if they made no typing errors because corrections were cumbersome to make and, in some legal professions, made documents invalid, is an interesting story that involves many different aspects of history.

The desire to work is almost innate. As German socialist Ferdinand Lassalle said in the 1850s, "Workingmen we all are so far as we have the desire to make ourselves useful to human society in any way whatever." Yet each historical period offers a million different stories of the history of each job and how it was performed. And that history is the history of human society.

Each book in the Working Life series strives to tell the tale of these anonymous workers. Primary source quotes offer veracity and immediacy to each volume, letting the workers themselves tell their stories. In addition, thorough bibliographies tell students where they can find out more information, and complete indexes allow for easy perusal of the text. While students learn about the work of years gone by, they gain empathy for those who toil and, perhaps, a universal pride in taking up the work that will someday be theirs.

POWER AND PRESTIGE: THE ORIGINS OF THE ROMAN SENATE

Today, the terms *senate* and *senator* conjure up visions of serious-looking, well-dressed men and women making speeches and debating in austere, marble-lined halls in Washington, D.C. The U.S. Senate is one of the two best known and prestigious legislative bodies in the world (the other being Britain's Parliament). The Senate discusses, amends, and passes laws formulated by members of the other branch of Congress (the House of Representatives), by the executive branch (the president), or by the senators themselves. It is clearly a high and singular honor, as well as a grave responsibility, to be a U.S. senator. Each of the one hundred senators serving in Washington wields a considerable amount of power and influence; the office of senator elicits immediate respect; and several senators have gone on to become president of the United States.

These integral facets of the job of senator—prestige, power, influence, responsibility, and respect—are not new, either to the present Senate or to modern legislatures in general. When America's founding fathers created the Senate under the articles of the U.S. Constitution, they desired that it possess all of these admirable qualities. And for inspiration, they looked back at a few outstanding historical models of strong representative legislatures (law-making bodies having at least some members who are elected). One was the British Parliament. Another was the Senate of ancient Rome.

The Roman Senate existed throughout most of the roughly twelve centuries of Rome's history as a nation-state (ca. 753 B.C.– A.D. 476). However, it was the role and authority of the Senate during the republican era of Rome (ca. 509–30 B.C.) that most impressed the American founders. (Following its collapse, the Roman Republic was replaced by the Roman Empire. The Empire was ruled by a series of emperors, and during this period the Senate had few powers and became more ceremonial in nature.)

Rome's leading republican senators were like old friends to Thomas Jefferson, Ben Franklin, James Madison, and the other American founders.

This was because classical history and culture, including Roman history and the Latin language, were compulsory components of the education of well-to-do young men in colonial America. They were steeped in the famous stories of noted ancient senators like Cato the Elder and Cicero. Jefferson and the others saw these men as heroic pillars of honest and

When Thomas Jefferson, Benjamin Franklin, and America's other founding fathers created their new government, they were inspired by the Roman Senate.

constructive representative government. The American founders could
also recite in detail the story of how
the Roman senators helped to establish the Republic and guided it in its
rise to power.

ROME'S FIRST SENATORS

That momentous story began in about
509 B.C. with the birth of the Republic. Before that time, Rome was ruled
by kings. What is known about the era
of the Roman Monarchy comes from
legends and old accounts collected by
later Greek writers, notably Polybius
(second century B.C.), Dionysius of
Halicarnassus (first century B.C.), and
Plutarch (first century A.D.), and Roman writers, notably Livy (first century B.C.). According to their accounts,
the founder of Rome, Romulus, was
also its first king. Livy tells how, after
laying out the city's defensive walls
and streets, Romulus made the first
laws and gathered around him the first
senators:

> He summoned his subjects and
> gave them laws, without which the
> creation of a unified [people]
> would have been impossible. In his
> view, the rabble [disorganized
> group] over which he ruled could
> be induced to respect the law only
> if he himself adopted certain visi-
> ble signs of power . . . of which the
> most important was the creation
> of the twelve lictors [men who car-

ried the fasces, the symbol of royal power] to attend his person. . . .
Romulus proceeded to temper
strength with policy and turned his
attention to social organization.
He created a hundred senators—
fixing that number either because
it was enough for his purpose, or
because there were no more than
a hundred who were in a position
to be made "fathers," as they were
so-called. The title of "fathers" un-
doubtedly was derived from their
rank, and their descendants were
called "patricians."[1]

This relatively brief quote by Livy
contains much vital information about
the early senators. First, they were
clearly leading and highly respected
citizens because they were called "fathers," in Latin *patres.* The *patres* and
their families and descendants made
up the noble patrician class (the term
patrician is derived from *patres*). The
patricians were all wealthy landown-
ers who enjoyed rights and privileges
superior to those of the commoners,
or plebs (short for plebeians), who
made up the bulk of the population.

But what did these initial one hundred senators do? In the same passage,
Livy talks about Romulus's "purpose"
for them, which must mean that they
served him in some capacity. This passage and other ancient evidence sug-
gest that these noblemen served as an
advisory board to the monarch, much

Romulus, Rome's legendary founder and first king, is mobbed by his followers. Rome's first senators served as a royal advisory board.

as American presidents have staffs of advisers today. The early senators apparently had other important functions as well, probably because of their high social rank. They acted as the king's cavalry when he was on military campaigns, for example. They also served as judges in legal disputes and as high priests who officiated at public sacrifices and told the king what he needed to do to appease the gods.

FOUNDING OF THE REPUBLIC

It is somewhat unclear how long the Roman Monarchy, with its advisory board of senators, lasted. The number of kings and the lengths of their reigns is also uncertain, but according to later tradition six more kings followed Romulus—Numa Pompilius, Tullus Hostilius, Ancus Marcius, Tarquinius Priscus, Servius Tullius, and Tarquinius Superbus (or "Tarquin the

An eighteenth-century engraving shows Lucius Junius Brutus officiating at the first meeting of the republican consuls and senators.

Proud"). Modern scholars think that a few of these men may have been only legendary and that there may have been other real kings whose names have not survived.

At any rate, all of the kings evidently chose senators as advisers, including the last, Tarquin, whose misrule helped bring about the fall of the Monarchy and establishment of the Republic. Tarquin already had a reputation as an unsavory character when he murdered King Servius Tullius and seized the throne. Then the new ruler arrested a number of patricians on phony charges so that he could take their wealthy estates for himself. This alienated many, if not most, of his senatorial advisers, who were themselves patricians. Finally, Tarquin's equally unprincipled son, Sextus, raped the wife of the noted patrician and patriot Lucius Tarquinius Collatinus. That proved to be the proverbial last straw for the patricians. Collatinus, helped by Lucius Junius Brutus and other leading noblemen, locked the Tarquins out of the city and dissolved the kingship.

The Roman fathers then proceeded to create a completely new kind of government, one based in considerable degree on the wishes and votes of the citizens. Clearly representative in nature, the system was highly enlightened for its time. Still, the Republic was not a true democracy, partly because only a minority of citizens could vote and hold public office. Meeting and voting in the citizen assemblies (*comitia*) was restricted to male citizens who could afford to own weapons and armor (which the average man could not afford to buy or make). Though not as esteemed as the patricians, these men were privileged. During assembly meetings they voted either to accept or reject new laws, as well as elected various high magistrates (public officials).

Among the leading magistrates were two consuls, administrator-generals who served jointly for one year. (Having two leaders serve short terms made it more difficult for any one man to amass excessive power.) Like the kings before them, they ran the government on a day-to-day basis and led the army in wartime. Also like the kings, the consuls needed advisers, preferably older, experienced men with high standing in social, political, and religious matters. The old advisory board of patrician senators was therefore retained.

THE SENATE BECOMES INDEPENDENT AND POWERFUL

The question is: How much authority did these senators wield in the early republican years? There is no doubt that by the end of the fourth century B.C., two centuries after the founding of the Republic, the Senate was by far the most powerful organ in the Roman government. According to Polybius:

> This body has control of the treasury and regulates the flow of all revenue and expenditure. . . . Any crimes committed in Italy which require public investigation, such as treason, conspiracy, poisoning, and assassination, also come under the jurisdiction of the Senate. Again, if any private person or community in Italy requires arbitration for a dispute, or is in need of formal censure, or seeks help or protection, it is the Senate which deals with all such cases. It is also responsible for dispatching embassies or commissions to countries outside Italy, either to settle differences, to offer advice, to impose demands, to receive submissions [surrenders], or to declare war. . . . All these matters are in the hands of the Senate and the people have nothing to do with them.[2]

In addition to these powers, the senators were extremely influential behind the scenes. They frequently set the political and social agendas of the consuls, for instance. Senators also routinely used their wealth and high position to sway members of the assembly to vote in a certain way.

Did the Senate possess all of this power and influence from the beginning? Did it even convene on a permanent basis in the early Republic? In the view of Polybius, Livy, Cicero, and their contemporaries, it did. But it is important to keep in mind that these men lived many centuries after the fact. They possessed no reliable historical documents describing the Senate from the era of the founders. And as noted classical scholar T.J. Cornell points out, the existence of a permanent, supremely powerful early Senate "may be based on no more than the unthinking assumption, which came naturally to . . . conservative political thinkers such as Cicero, that the Senate had always been an important part of the Roman political system."[3]

In fact, a number of modern scholars think it is probable that the Senate remained mainly an impermanent advisory body for more than a century after the Republic's founding. In this view, at first the consuls chose the senators and decided when they would meet. Over time, however, the senators acquired increasing authority and influence. The major turning point seems to have been the passage of the Lex Ovinia sometime between 339 and 332 B.C. This law established a set procedure for enrolling ex-magistrates in the Senate, eliminating the senators' dependence on and direct control by the consuls; the law also ensured that, once enrolled, a senator would serve for life.

The Senate thereby became an independent and permanent body. And as Cornell says, "it gradually acquired

A herald (with staff) leads a group of foreign dignitaries to meet with key members of the early Roman Senate (sitting on the platform).

its control of the government in the generations following the passage of the Lex Ovinia."[4] For the next three centuries, the position and work of a senator was both honored and crucial in the Roman world. Moreover, the precedent of the Senate as a body endowed with high prestige and moral, as well as political, authority was set for future ages and nations.

CHAPTER 1

BECOMING A ROMAN SENATOR

Modern Americans pride themselves on having a government with three branches (executive, legislative, and judicial), each of which balances and checks the powers of the others. The ancient Roman Republic also had three major branches that, at least in theory, were supposed to balance one another. These were the consuls; the Senate; and the people, (who met in their assemblies, the *comitia*). According to Polybius:

> All the aspects of the [Roman government's] administration were, taken separately, so fairly and so suitably ordered and regulated through the agency of these three elements that it was impossible even for the Romans themselves to declare with certainty whether the whole system was an aristocracy, a democracy, or a monarchy. In fact, it was quite natural that

this be so, for if we were to fix our eyes only upon the power of the consuls, the constitution might give the impression of being completely monarchical and royal; if we confined our attention to the Senate, it would seem to be aristocratic; and if we looked at the power of the people, it would appear to be a clear example of democracy.[5]

In truth, during mid-to-late republican times these three main elements of Rome's government rarely struck a true balance. This was because the Senate was almost always more powerful and influential than the other two elements in those years. Yet thanks to the wisdom of the Republic's founding fathers, the Senate remained intertwined with and to some degree dependent on the consuls and popular assemblies. And working together, the three governmental branches clearly had the potential to accomplish great deeds. "This peculiar form of constitution," Polybius writes, "possesses an irresistible power to achieve any goal it has set itself."[6]

Because of the prominence of the Senate in the Roman government and the vital work that powerful legislature did for the Roman nation, the position of senator was the most prestigious public office a man could hold in Rome. (Women had no political rights and had no chance of becoming senators or other magistrates.) Senators were generally wealthy, well-educated, politically astute, dedicated to serving the nation, and responsible for the welfare of millions of people. Therefore, choosing senators was a serious matter. The process was highly formal, and candidates had to meet requirements so stringent that only a tiny percentage of Romans ever had a chance of making it into the honored senatorial ranks.

THE LADDER OF SERVICE

The exact manner in which senators were chosen in the first century or so of the Republic is somewhat unclear. What is more certain is that after the passage of the Lex Ovinia in the 330s B.C. men were enrolled into the Senate by important public officials called censors. Two men who served jointly for five-year terms, the censors periodically conducted censuses of prop-

erty owners and their holdings. This produced lists containing the names of all citizens, rich and poor, along with their approximate net worth. The censors also oversaw public morality, supervised the leasing of public land, and decided which new public construction projects would be funded.

It seemed appropriate to the Romans that the censors should oversee senatorial enrollment, too. They believed that men charged with the delicate task of keeping a close watch on the citizenry, its ethics, and the way it used its most precious commodity—its land—could also be trusted to regulate entry into its most powerful governmental body. In theory, the censors were supposed to enroll senators from among the "best" men in society. But what qualities made a person one of the best? In the early years of the Republic, a candidate had to be a patrician, which meant that he belonged to the traditional ancient nobility and was wealthy, with money derived from land ownership and management.

Over time it became customary for the censors to allow former consuls and other major ex-magistrates to become senators. In this way, appointment to the Senate became partly a reward for earlier service to the state. At some point, perhaps when the Ovinian law passed, it became an actual requirement; after that, all prospective senators had to be former magistrates in high public offices.

❧ THE OFFICE OF CENSOR ❧

Entry into the Senate was dependent on the censors (in Latin *censores*), who held one of the most important and prestigious of the major magistracies of the Roman Republic. The citizenry (meeting in one of their assemblies) elected two censors every five years, which meant that these officials held their positions five times longer than the consuls. The duties of the censors were to conduct a census of property owners and their holdings; to make and maintain lists of all citizens; to oversee public morality; to prepare lists of proposed senators and remove corrupt senators; to supervise the leasing of public land; to decide on new public construction projects; and to award contracts for such projects. In the early Empire, the emperors assumed most of the powers of the censors, whose office thereafter ceased to be of any real importance and became mostly ceremonial.

A censor (seated) questions two citizens about their conduct. The censors oversaw public morality.

Once in the Senate, they served in it for life.

These public offices that produced the candidates for the Senate collectively formed an ascending ladder of governmental service known as the *cursus honorum* (literally translated as the "course of honors"). For a long time men followed the *cursus* simply out of respect for cherished custom. But it was finally fixed by law in 180 B.C. Usually, the sequence began with

service in the army, although this was technically not part of the *cursus* proper. Then came the office of quaestor. The quaestors were financial officers who administered the public treasury, acted as paymasters for the army, and managed the finances of the realm's growing number of provinces.

The high offices that followed that of quaestor were aedile (which was optional), praetor, consul, and censor. These were known as "curule" magistracies because those men holding them were entitled to use a special "chair of state" called the *sella curulis.* The first man in a family to attain a curule magistracy (particularly the consulship) was given the prestigious title of *novus homo,* or "new man." The duties of these curule officers were as follows. The aediles were in charge of maintaining and repairing public structures, overseeing public markets (including weights and measures), and organizing public games and festivals. Praetors were high-level judges who oversaw the courts, and the censors kept watch on public morality. The consuls always became senators after their year of service (if they were not in the Senate already). Cicero describes their pivotal office, along with the special office of dictator (to be filled in a national emergency):

> There shall . . . be two officials with the power that used to belong to the kings. . . . It is "consuls" that they will be habitually called. While on military service they will be invested with supreme authority. There shall be no one above them. Their dominant preoccupation shall be the welfare of the people.

No one [consul] shall occupy the same office twice, except after an interval of ten years duration. . . . When, however, a serious war occurs, or civil strife, a single man shall be invested with the power that normally belongs to the two consuls, if the Senate so decrees.

Wearing a colored cloak over his toga, a quaestor reaches for his financial ledger.

But this dictatorship shall not last longer than six months.[7]

Any young man of substance who wanted to have a successful political career was expected to serve in the lowest of these offices first and work his way to the top. However, some individuals did not follow the exact sequence of the *cursus;* also, a man did not have to serve in all the public offices in question to gain entry into the Senate. As long as he had been at least a quaestor, the censors could, providing his character was good, consider him for the Senate.

THE PLEBS' STRUGGLE TO BECOME SENATORS

This ladder of public service that almost always gained a man entry into the Senate was all well and good for the patricians, who at first held a virtual stranglehold on governmental power and social influence in Rome. The requirement that a person had to be a patrician to become a senator ensured that the purity and exclusivity of patrician order (here meaning social class) would be perpetuated. However, the plebs quite naturally felt left out. Though some of their number could attend and vote in the popular assemblies, no member of the plebeian order could become a praetor, a consul, a censor, or a senator. The plebs increasingly objected to this unfair situation.

The result was a protracted series of public protests and political struggles generally referred to as the "Conflict of the Orders." These struggles began in about 494 B.C., when the plebs pressed their demands for change by going on strike and refusing to serve in the military. "In Rome there was something like a panic," Livy recalls.

> With one party as much alarmed by the situation as the other, everything came to a standstill. The commons [plebs] . . . feared violence at the hands of the senatorial party, who, in their turn, were afraid of the commons. . . . What would happen if, in the present situation, there was a threat of foreign invasion? Clearly, the only hope lay in finding a solution for the conflicting interests of the two classes.[8]

Feeling they had no other choice, therefore, the patricians gave in. They agreed to let the plebs elect officers known as tribunes of the people, plebeian officials who had veto power over the passage of laws and acts formulated by the patrician consuls and senators. The tribunes, says Livy, were in a real sense "above the law," and their main function was "to protect the commons against the consuls [and senators]." In addition, "no man of the senatorial class was allowed" to become a tribune.[9] That way the plebs could be certain that men of their own class were looking out for their interests.

In the late 490s B.C., three tribunes argue with a military officer. The tribunes were plebeian officials with veto power over senatorial legislation.

The Conflict of the Orders continued on a sporadic basis for several more generations. About 450 B.C., the plebs demanded that the laws governing society be written down, which resulted in the great legal codification known as the Twelve Tables. Soon afterward, the hard-fought passage of a law called the Lex Canuleia gave plebs the right to marry patricians, including senators. In 409 B.C., the first plebeian quaestors were elected, giving commoners access to at least the lowest office in the coveted *cursus honorum*. And in 366 B.C., the plebs won the final phase of their long struggle when they gained the right to run for and serve as consul. (Thereafter, it became customary for one of the two serving consuls to be a patrician and the other a pleb.)

The plebs' admittance to the consulship had a crucial indirect impact on the makeup of the Senate, changing the prerequisites needed for entry. As Robert C. Byrd explains in his book about the Roman Senate:

> Once plebeians gained admission to the consulship, they could no longer be barred from the other higher magistracies, such as the dictatorship or the censorship. And as it had long been the custom that ex-consuls, and later ex-praetors, were to be enrolled in the

The people rejoice as the Twelve Tables are displayed. Writing down the laws emphasized that all Romans, regardless of class, were bound by them.

Senate's membership, the attainment of these higher magistracies meant an ever-increasing representation in the Senate by the plebeians.[10]

DIFFERING VIEWS OF WHAT CONSTITUTED HONORABLE WORK

Whether they were of patrician or plebeian birth, senators had certain status, privileges, and educational backgrounds in common, all of which were unusual or special as compared with average Romans. First, all were rich. Even the plebs who made it into the Senate were wealthy men because they could not have gained the consulship or other high offices in the first place without connections to powerful, well-to-do people and years of financial success. That success was usually the result of owning land, but sometimes it came from trade or other business dealings.

Once in the Senate, however, a man was not allowed to engage in trade, banking, shop-keeping, or other forms of commerce, let alone ordinary physical labor. Members of the aristocratic class, who still largely controlled the Senate, viewed such activities as bordering on disreputable and definitely beneath their dignity. Most people today would see this attitude as arrogant and counter to a good work ethic. But dozens of generations of custom had drilled it into the psyche of Rome's upper classes, so even a man as honest, fair, and hardworking as Cicero accepted it as a fact of life. His statement of this unwritten law followed by all senators during the Republic is the best known of any Roman writer. "Now as for crafts and other means of livelihood," it begins,

the following is roughly what we have been told [by our ancestors and tradition] as to which should be thought fit for a free man, and which demeaning [or vulgar]. First, those means of livelihood that incur the dislike of other men are not approved, for example, collecting harbor dues, or usury [money lending]. Again, all those workers who are paid for their [manual] labor and not for their skill have servile and demeaning employment; for in their case the very wage [they receive] is a contract to servitude. Those who buy from merchants and sell again immediately should also be thought of as demeaning themselves. For they would make no profit unless they told sufficient lies, and nothing is more dishonorable than falsehood. All handcraftsmen are engaged in a demeaning trade; for there can be nothing well bred about the workshop. The crafts that are least worthy of approval are those that minister to the pleasures, [including] fishmongers, butchers, cooks . . . fishermen . . . perfumers, dancers, and the whole variety show [theatrical acts and displays].[11]

It remains somewhat unclear where Roman senators and other high-placed Romans acquired this condescending attitude toward the trades and manual labor in general. Perhaps the fact that traditionally such jobs were filled almost exclusively by poor, uneducated people and slaves made them appear degrading to the upper classes. Another factor was that most free Romans, even most poor ones, came to feel that taking orders from someone else was the act of a slave. As a noted scholar of ancient slavery, Keith Hopkins, phrases it:

> Free-born Roman citizens traditionally disliked the idea of working as long-term employees at the beck and call of other free men (except in the army). . . . [They] apparently felt that a permanent job restricted their freedom of choice [and] constrained them like slaves.[12]

CICERO DEFINES THE IDEAL SENATOR

The consequences of these singular attitudes toward work held by Roman society in general and the Senate in particular were major and in some ways counterproductive and detrimental. Because of the upper-class prejudice against the trades and menial professions, most Roman tradesmen, craftsmen, and business and industrial workers were slaves or freedmen (former slaves who had gained their freedom). A majority of Romans even shunned "servile" positions in administration, including the staffs of the senators, consuls, praetors, and provincial governors (and even the emperors during the Empire). The senators and other high-ranking figures paid most of these workers wages but refused to take money for their own services.

In this way, among others, senators and other magistrates maintained a status distinct from and superior to that of common laborers and slaves. Men like Cicero saw and routinely portrayed themselves as generous, civic-minded, patriotic individuals who had chosen to sacrifice their valuable time and energy to the service of their country and the people of Rome. This was only the ideal, of course. In reality, some senators were selfish, or greedy, or ambitious, or cared more about promoting their own interests than serving the country.

Yet others did their best to live up to the ideal. One who certainly did was Cicero. Often in his voluminous writings he advocates the idea of the wealthy and powerful, especially senators like

❧ Cicero: Champion of the Republic ❧

Modern scholars know more about Marcus Tullius Cicero than about any other person of the ancient world. This is partly because he was an eminent lawyer, orator, senator, and patriot who played a key role in the last years of the Roman Republic. Even more so it is because he generated an enormous literary output, most of which has survived. It includes fifty-eight lengthy speeches, over eight hundred letters, and some two thousand pages of philosophical and rhetorical tracts, constituting a treasure trove of information about himself, his friends, his society, and the Roman character.

Cicero was born in 106 B.C. and received a first-rate education. He served as quaestor in 75 B.C., aedile in 69, praetor in 66, consul in 63, and senator from 74 to 43. Many Romans admired Cicero for upholding old-fashioned republican values of honesty, unselfish service to the state, and duty to country. But he was unable to save the Republic from the deterioration caused by years of civil war and power struggles among ambitious generals such as Caesar, Pompey, and Antony. Time and again Cicero found his efforts to defend the Senate's authority impeded by these men. And eventually his name appeared at the top of their list of enemies. In 43 B.C., Antony ordered soldiers to assassinate the great senator, whose head and hands were nailed to a platform in Rome's main square. In the eyes of many in later generations, the Republic and its noblest qualities and ideals died with Cicero.

A bust of Cicero, one of the greatest orators and legislators of the ancient world is pictured.

himself, using at least some of their personal and financial largess to benefit the people and the nation. "The achievements which are greatest and show the greatest spirit," he writes in the treatise *On Duties*,

are those of the men who rule the Republic [i.e., the magistrates and senators]. For their government reaches extremely widely and affects the greatest number. Many men of great spirit, however, have lived and still live lives of leisure. Some . . . have taken a middle course between philosophy and the administration of the Republic. . . . Their wealth should in the

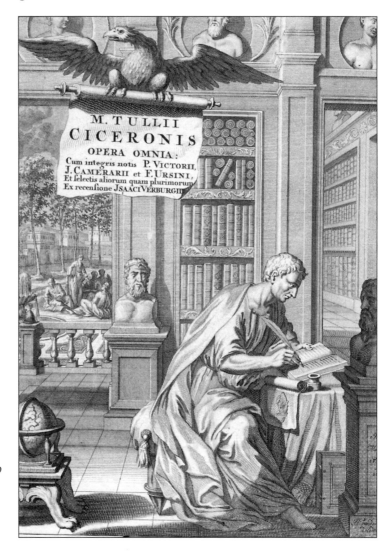

A late medieval engraving depicts Cicero at work. He was known for his intelligence, diligence, dignity, and sense of fair play.

first place be well won, and not dishonorably . . . acquired. Secondly, it should be increased by reason, industriousness, and thrift. Thirdly, it should be available for the benefit of as many [people] as possible, provided they are worthy of it, and be at the command not of lust and luxury, but of liberality [in honest government service] and [charity]. A man who observes these rules may live not only in a grand, impressive, and spirited manner, but also with simplicity and trustworthiness, a true friend of other men.[13]

SPECIAL PRIVILEGES

Wealth and freedom from ordinary sorts of labor were not the only privileges that went with a Roman senator's high political and social status. Even a senator's mode of dress was special. When in public or at a session in the Senate House, he wore a distinctive toga, the *toga praetexta*, which featured a purple stripe along its edges. (Purple was the color associated with royalty in ancient times.) This toga was reserved for curule magistrates only, which included consuls and praetors as well as senators. To make senators stand out even more from the other curule magistrates, the senator's toga had a conspicuously broader stripe, called the *latus clavus*. A senator also wore a special kind of shoe, a

sandal dyed red and fastened by long straps that wound around and up his leg.

A senator's outfit easily singled him out in a crowd. And people who encountered senators in the streets, forum (town square), marketplace, courts, or other public places were expected, out of respect, to make way for them. Likewise, senators were automatically allowed to sit in the best seats at any public event. They even had permanent, exclusive seating sections set aside for them in theaters, amphitheaters (stadiums that featured gladiatorial bouts and wild-animal shows), and circuses (facilities for horse and chariot races). (The exception was during the Empire, when the emperor and his family had slightly better seats than the senators.) Any ordinary citizen who dared to sit in a senator's seat faced arrest and punishment.

EDUCATIONAL AND PROFESSIONAL BACKGROUND

Another mark of a senator's distinction was his educational background and professional experiences. Because almost all senators came from wealthy families, they could afford the best educations, which gave them an immediate head start in life. After graduating from secondary school, men of substance usually went on to study with highly reputed instructors of law and rhetoric (the art of persuasive speaking). Such knowledge and skills were deemed essential for any young man who aspired to a career in one or both of the most prestigious professions—lawyer and politician.

The art of rhetoric was particularly important because the ability to compose and effectively deliver speeches was absolutely essential to success in both law and politics. In an era without television, radio, newspapers, and the Internet, the most effective way to reach and gain the support of the populace was through public oratory. The power of this kind of speaking was especially evident in the courts. There, a well-trained, experienced lawyer with a talent for oratory could get a guilty client off simply by winning over the jury with a well-crafted speech delivered with finesse and much emotional passion. Likewise, senators like Cicero and his famous contemporaries Marcus Brutus and Cato the Younger often swayed their fellows in the Senate through grandiose speeches that manipulated or inflamed their emotions.

Cicero's educational and professional background was a case in point. As a young man he was tutored by the legendary orator Apollonius Molo (from the Greek island of Rhodes), who taught him rhetoric. Cicero also studied with the greatest lawyer of his era, Mucius Scaevola.

Thanks to these men, Cicero's enormous personal talents matured rapidly and he rose to public prominence much faster than most of his contemporaries who also sought careers in law and politics. In 80 B.C., when he was twenty-six, Cicero made a big splash by winning his first big case. (His client was a man named Roscius, who had been accused of killing his own father.) Only five years later, Cicero attained the first step in the *cursus honorum* (quaestor), and in 74 B.C., at the age of only thirty-two, Cicero took his seat in the Senate, which he was destined to hold with extraordinary distinction for thirty-one years.

REMOVING SENATORS

During the Republic, there were only two ways that Cicero or any other senator could be removed from his senatorial seat. One was by dying, which is the way Cicero himself ended his career. (Actually, he was murdered by the henchmen of a political enemy, Mark Antony, during the Republic's last days.) The other way was when a senator committed some serious offense against the state, such as treason. In such a case the censors stepped in, weighed the evidence against the senator, and, if they were satisfied that he was guilty, removed him from the rolls and replaced him. (In the Empire, by contrast, the emperor could remove members of the Senate for whatever

❧ THE ROMAN TOGA ❧

The toga, the garment that all senators wore to their meetings, was the most prominent and fashionable article of outdoor clothing worn by Roman men. It came to symbolize the peaceful citizen, as opposed to the soldier in his armor. In fact, during the early Republic only citizens were allowed to wear it, although this restriction was later dropped. The toga consisted of an oblong piece of cloth, about nineteen feet long, that was wrapped around the body to create various folds and drapes. Different kinds of togas denoted social or political rank or status. An average citizen wore the plain off-white or brown *toga alba.* Pure white togas were reserved for political candidates to make them stand out in a crowd. Senators and other high officials wore the *toga praetexta,* which featured a purple border. A victorious general (and later the emperors) donned the all-purple, gold-trimmed *toga picta.* And mourners attending a funeral put on the black *toga pulla.*

Surviving statues show two of the many ways the Romans wrapped their togas.

Cicero and many other senators made their names in courts like this one, where the power of oratory was an overriding factor.

reason he saw fit.) As it was, very few senators were ever removed for wrongdoing. Once a man had made it into the most prestigious political body in the known world, he was unlikely to risk losing a position of power, privilege, and honor that most people could only dream about.

CHAPTER 2

DOMESTIC POWERS OF SENATORS

The amount of power and authority wielded by the Senate during the mid- to late Republic was impressive, even staggering. Some of the authority the senators possessed was in the area of foreign affairs, which quite literally depended on their decisions and decrees. No less crucial, however, were the roles the senators played in domestic affairs, which can be generally defined as those taking place in and directly affecting the lives of the inhabitants of Italy, the Roman heartland. In that geographical sphere, the Senate controlled the flow of state funds. It prepared or amended legislation for the popular assemblies to vote on. The senators maintained domestic security by funding and helping to direct the strategies of the army. And they played major roles in supervising the state religion. Clearly, this small group of wealthy, privileged individuals had a direct or indirect hand in practically all important domestic realms.

A WIDE RANGE OF POWERS

This does not mean that the Senate was all-powerful in the republican government. The senators were somewhat constrained by some minor checks and balances built into the Republic's constitutional system. Polybius addressed this reality, saying that although the Senate possessed great power, it was

obliged first of all to pay attention in public affairs to the views of the people and to respect their wishes. . . . For if anyone introduces a law which aims to remove from the Senate some of its traditional authority, or to abolish the precedence [superiority] or other dignities of the senators, or even to reduce some of their property, in all such cases it is the people alone who are empowered to pass the measure or to reject it.[14]

In other words, a law or edict passed by the voters in a popular assembly could impede the will, workings, and authority of the Senate. In fact, if no public magistrate called for a meeting of the Senate, its members could not even convene to do their work.

At least this is how the senators might be limited and constrained in theory. In actual practice, it was very difficult for a popular politician to muster enough votes to challenge the

This drawing is based on an eroded sculpture showing Roman men lined up to vote. Senators often influenced how citizens voted.

Senate's authority. Enormous numbers of ordinary Roman voters knew a senator personally, or they or their families were beholden to him for some prior favors. As a result, it was highly unlikely that a majority of voters would overrule the Senate in a given situation. Also, there were always at least a few strong senatorial supporters among the public magistrates

(some of whom were senators themselves); this ensured that someone would call for a meeting of the senators whenever they so desired.

As Polybius pointed out, the senators had less to fear from the voters and more from the tribunes who possessed veto powers under the constitution. "If a single one of the tribunes interposes his veto," Polybius writes,

the Senate is not only prevented from reaching a final decision on any subject, but cannot meet and hold sittings. Now the tribunes are always bound to carry out the decrees of the people, and above all, to pay attention to their wishes. For all these reasons, therefore, the Senate stands in awe of the masses and takes heed of the popular will.[15]

Because the tribunes held such potential power over the senators, it became common for senators to get on the good side of at least some of the tribunes. It was not unusual for tribunes to be wined and dined, have their debts paid, or even receive out-and-out bribes by members of the Senate in an effort to dissuade them from using their veto power in critical matters.

Ultimately, though, it was not primarily favors and bribes that made moves by the tribunes and assemblies against the Senate only short-term in their impact. It was the Senate's wide range of powers and the large number of societal niches the senators penetrated and shaped. Put another way, the reach of the senators into domestic political and social affairs was so long and strong that nothing short of naked force could dislodge it in the long run. (And in fact, it was the very use of such force against the Senate that brought down the Republic in the late first century B.C.)

AUTHORIZING MONEY FOR CONTRACTORS

The extensive powers and reach of the senators in domestic affairs is best illustrated by the Senate's supremacy in state financial matters. The senators managed the treasury; paid the soldiers, contractors, and laborers; and distributed huge amounts of public funds for a wide range of projects across the length and breadth of Italy. The quaestors kept the records and made the actual payments, but these officials were obliged at all times to follow the directives of the senators. Similarly, the censors decided which new structures would be built and chose the contractors to do the work; however, the Senate authorized the money, without which no project could proceed. According to Polybius:

> This body [the Senate] has control of the treasury and regulates the flow of all revenue and expenditure. The quaestors require a de-

cree of the Senate to enable them to authorize expenditure on any given project, with the exception only of payments made to the consuls. The Senate also controls what is by far the largest and most important item of expenditure—that is, the program which is laid down by the censors every five years to provide for the repair and construction of public buildings—and it makes a grant to the censors for this purpose.[16]

In another passage, Polybius provides more detail about the ways the Senate controlled contractors. These mostly well-to-do men headed the companies that erected the temples, courts, amphitheaters, roads, aqueducts, and other state-sponsored structures, as well as collected all manner of revenues to replenish the state treasury. "All over Italy," Polybius begins,

> an immense number of contracts, far too numerous to specify, are awarded by the censors for the construction and repair of public buildings, and besides this the collection of revenues from navigable rivers, harbors, gardens, mines, lands—in a word every transaction which comes under the control of the Roman government—is farmed out to contractors. . . . There is scarcely a soul, one might say, who does not have some in-

❧ POLYBIUS ON THE SENATE ❧ AND THE MILITARY

In this passage from his Histories, *Polybius explains the major ways that the senators exerted influence over the army, the generals, and domestic security.*

The legions [army battalions] require a constant flow of supplies, but without the approval of the Senate neither corn nor clothing nor pay can be provided, so that a commander's plans can be completely frustrated if the Senate chooses to be unsympathetic or obstructive. It also rests with the Senate to decide whether a general can execute all his plans and designs, since it has the right either to send out another general when the former's term of office has expired, or to retain him in command for another year. Again, it is in the power of the Senate either to celebrate a general's successes with pomp and magnify them, or to obscure and belittle them. For the processions which they call triumphs, in which the spectacle of what they [the generals] have achieved in the field is actually brought before the eyes of their fellow-citizens, cannot be properly staged, or in some cases enacted at all, unless the Senate agrees and grants the necessary funds.

terest in these contracts and the profits which are derived from them. . . . All these transactions come under the authority of the Senate. It can grant an extension of time, it can lighten the contractor's liability [responsibility to make restitution] in the event of some unfortunate accident, or release him altogether if it proves impossible for him to fulfill his contract. There are in fact many ways in which the Senate can either inflict great hardship or ease the burden for those who manage public property, for in every case the appeal is referred to it.[17]

STRUGGLES OVER CONTROL OF THE TREASURY

The money the Senate authorized for such projects came directly from the state treasury, in which large amounts of gold and silver coins were stored. That treasury, known as the *Aerarium Populi Romani* ("Treasury of the Roman People"), was located in the Temple of Saturn (a very ancient and important agricultural god). The temple was located on a slope (perhaps near the base) of Rome's Capitoline Hill (often called simply "the Capitol"), which was viewed as sacred because it was dominated by a complex of temples. Two quaestors were headquartered

The Temple of Saturn, which housed the treasury, was located at the far end of Rome's main Forum, seen here as it looked in the late Republic.

there to watch over the money for the senators. (The quaestors also guarded an antique scale, a museum piece from Rome's early years when money had taken the form of cumbersome bronze and iron bars that had to be weighed during each transaction.)

The treasury in the temple was vital to the Senate and the government overall; neither could function for very long without access to state funds to pay the soldiers, construction workers, firefighters, and other essential personnel. On at least one occasion, an opponent of the senators and their policies tried to use their access to the treasury against them. Plutarch documented this attempt to block the Senate's ac-

cess to the treasury in a passage in his biography of the noted second-century-B.C. social and political reformer Tiberius Sempronius Gracchus. Gracchus had proposed a new law that would distribute tracts of public land to poor farmers. Most senators were against it because they wanted rich people, including themselves, to get the bulk of the land. When his opponents tried to stop the law from passing, Gracchus, then a tribune, used his veto powers. He began issuing vetoes (which took the form of official edicts) designed to bring the work of the Senate to a halt. In this way, according to Plutarch, Gracchus prohibited not only the senators but also:

all the other magistrates from transacting any public business until the people had cast their votes either for or against his law. He also placed his private seal [symbol of the office of tribune] on the Temple of Saturn so as to prevent the quaestors from drawing money out of the treasury or paying it in. [The seal was almost certainly accompanied by armed guards.] At the same time, he gave public notice that a penalty would be imposed [by the people's assembly] upon any praetor [or other official] who disobeyed the edict. The result of this was to alarm the magistrates so much that they suspended all their various functions.[18]

This tactic of using the tribune's veto power to shut down the government worked in the short run, for Gracchus's bill soon passed in the assembly. However, the senators had the last word, since in the long run they held the financial reins of the Roman state. The Senate later refused to pay

Tiberius Gracchus places his seal on the door of the Temple of Saturn. Unfortunately for him, the senators retaliated by instigating a riot.

the group of men commissioned to implement the land redistribution. (Also, a group of senators instigated a riot at a meeting Gracchus was holding, leaving the tribune and a hundred of his supporters dead. Later generations of Romans viewed Gracchus and his brother, Gaius, who was also murdered after instituting social reforms, as heroes.)

THE SENATE AND RELIGION

In addition to its financial power, the Senate was extremely influential in religious matters. For one thing, the senators sometimes met in temples (before the Senate House was built, when it was being renovated, or for other reasons). More important, though, was the relationship between the Senate and the pontiffs (*pontifices*) of the state religion. (This was the ancient faith that recognized Jupiter as the chief god of a pantheon that included Mars, Neptune, Juno, Minerva, and other deities.) There were probably originally three pontiffs who served jointly. But by the late Republic, that number had increased to sixteen. The most important and prestigious pontiff was the *pontifex maximus*, Rome's chief priest.

The pontiffs had a number of tasks, which were sanctioned by and sometimes directed by the senators. One was to determine the dates of religious festivals (which varied from year to year). Another was to decide on which

days it was all right for people to conduct legal business. The pontiffs also kept records of major religious and political events. All of these duties were important to the continued smooth running of the state and society, and keeping a watchful eye over them was a way for the Senate to maintain its control over the government and the people.

In this way, the state religion became in a sense a department of the government. Priests came to be elected. And the senators and pontiffs, who had much in common, worked closely with one another. In fact, most state priests were patricians, and many of them were senators as well as priests. For this reason, senators tended to wield a disproportionate amount of influence and authority in state religious affairs.

The senators could even ban certain religious practices that they deemed a threat to public order. This happened in 186 B.C. Followers of the fertility god Bacchus (the Roman equivalent of the Greek god Dionysus) had been growing more numerous. They often staged public processions in which people wore masks and used obscene language. They also conducted secret ceremonies called Bacchanalia. And the conservative senators heard rumors that these rites had degenerated into drunken orgies (a charge that was either untrue or greatly exaggerated). Accordingly,

❧ GODS AND PRIESTS ☙
OF THE STATE RELIGION

Rome's state religion, over which the senators had much influence, promoted the traditional pantheon (group of gods) worshiped in the early centuries of the Republic. These deities included the chief god Jupiter, whose main temple, on the Capitoline Hill, was seen as the heart of the state religion. Other major members of the state pantheon were Juno, Jupiter's wife and protector of women and childbirth; Minerva, goddess of war and protector of craftsmen; Mercury, Jupiter's messenger, who protected travelers and tradesmen; Vesta, goddess of the hearth; and Mars, god of war.

Formal worship of these gods was overseen by priests, who were not full-time spiritual guides in the modern sense. Most Roman priests were men of high social status who received training in religious matters and then executed their religious duties on a part-time basis. The various kinds of priests were organized into groups called "colleges." The college of the high priests, the pontiffs, for example, was known as the *collegium pontificum*. Other kinds of priests included the augurs and haruspices, who interpreted divine signs by observing the behavior of birds or the entrails of sacrificial animals, and the *fetiales*, who oversaw rituals regarding foreign relations, such as making treaties and declaring war. There were also a few priestesses, principally the Vestal Virgins, who tended the sacred fire on the state hearth.

*An engraving depicts the high pontiff (*pontifex maximus*) officiating at an altar in a public sacrifice.*

the Senate prohibited the Bacchanalia in all of Italy. (Despite the ban, the cult of Bacchus eventually revived and enjoyed considerable popularity during the early Empire.)

THE SENATE VERSUS HANNIBAL

The senators' authority was no less far-reaching in matters of domestic security. True, the consuls actually com-

---

☽ HANNIBAL, ENEMY OF ROME ☾

One of the most formidable of all the foes the Roman Senate and the military machine it controlled ever faced was Hannibal, who led the main Carthaginian forces in the Second Punic War (fought between Rome and Carthage from 218 to 201 B.C.). According to Livy and other ancient historians, Hannibal's father, Hamilcar Barca, hated the Romans after Carthage's defeat in the First Punic War (264–241 B.C.) and passed on that hatred to his young son. In 219 B.C., after Hamilcar's death, the grown Hannibal attacked Saguntum, Rome's only ally in Spain, and Rome declared war. Hannibal then surprised the Romans by crossing his army over the Alps into northern Italy.

The Carthaginians won a stunning series of victories, including the one at Cannae (in 216 B.C.), in which eighty senators were among the fifty thousand Romans killed. However, Hannibal was unable to follow up effectively on these victories. Most of Rome's Italian allies, whom Hannibal had hoped would come over to his side, remained loyal. In 202 B.C., Hannibal finally suffered defeat at the hands of the Roman general Pub-

lius Cornelius Scipio at Zama, in North Africa. The peace was signed in 201 B.C. In the years that followed, the Romans hunted Hannibal down until he committed suicide in 183 B.C.

A nineteenth-century woodcut shows Hannibal leading his army across the Alps.

manded the armies, with which they carried out any defensive or offensive measures necessary to protect Rome and other Italian towns from attack. Yet the senators regularly advised the consuls in most affairs, especially military ones. The Senate also paid the soldiers' salaries and provided the money for their food, uniforms, and other supplies.

There were also military emergencies in which the Senate could and did act. At times, for instance, the armed forces had to be divided into several contingents to meet threats on multiple fronts, so more than two commanders were needed; or one or more consuls or other generals might be killed or incapacitated and had to be replaced immediately. In such situations the Senate appointed the required military officers and gave them their marching orders. Noted scholar F.R. Cowell sums up the extensive national security powers the senators held:

> The civil authority of the Senate was accepted without question as being superior to the military power of the senior magistrates and the army. It [the Senate] found money to equip and supply armies in the field and men to reinforce them. Whenever, in the great age of the Republic, it became necessary to maintain more armies in the provinces than the consuls

could control, the Senate assigned the additional commander to his post. It was to the Senate that the army commanders sent their reports and it was the Senate by whom they were reprimanded, recalled, or given the much coveted distinction of a public triumph [victory parade] through the streets of Rome. It was to the Senate that the troops looked for their share of booty and a grant of public land, a Roman equivalent of a military pension.[19]

One type of security situation the Senate had to deal with was when a foreign enemy invaded Italian soil and directly threatened the Roman state and people. Perhaps the most dramatic example was when the great Carthaginian general Hannibal crossed the Alps in 218 B.C. with an invasion force and descended into the Italian peninsula. (Rome had recently declared war on Carthage, a city and empire centered in what is now Tunisia, in North Africa.) In the months that followed, the senators met on a regular basis and received constant word, via messengers, about the enemy's movements.

The exact advice the Senate gave the consuls during this crisis is unknown. But there is no doubt that the senators coordinated the overall strategy of the war effort. They appointed and recalled generals as they saw fit.

And as Livy later wrote, after Hannibal had won a series of victories north of Rome, "the praetors kept the Senate sitting from sunrise to sunset for several days, to debate the question of what leader they could find and what forces they could raise to continue resistance against the victorious enemy."[20] Many people thought Hannibal would soon march directly on the city of Rome, so the constitutional provision for appointing a dictator in an extreme national emergency was invoked. Quintus Fabius Maximus was chosen, along with an assistant (called the "Master of the Horse"), Marcus Minucius Rufus. According to Livy:

> The two men were entrusted by the Senate with the task of strengthening the defenses of the city walls, posting garrisons [groups of soldiers] wherever they

A Roman officer greets the newly appointed dictator, Quintus Fabius Maximus.

should see fit, and destroying the bridges [leading across the Tiber River into the city]. The defense of Italy had failed, [so the senators decided that] the war henceforward would be . . . to save the city.[21]

The Senate's pivotal role in the war against Hannibal was evident later, too. After Fabius's term as dictator expired in 216 B.C., new consuls were elected. And the Senate approved a plan to put them in joint command of the largest Roman army ever assembled—more than seventy thousand men. The senators and consuls were confident they could defeat Hannibal, who had only forty thousand men, in a single decisive knock-out blow. Just the opposite occurred, however. Hannibal won a tremendous victory at Cannae (in southeastern Italy), killing more than fifty thousand Romans, including some eighty senators. Once more, the Senate faced the task of organizing the immediate defense of the city, since it was assumed that Hannibal would follow up his win by besieging the capital. (He surprised them by not doing so, however, and the Romans were eventually able to rebound and win the war.)

THE SENATE VERSUS SPARTACUS

Another kind of domestic military emergency the Senate had to deal with was when a group of slaves rebelled and threatened the security of the Roman state and people. The trouble began in 73 B.C. A group of gladiators at a training school in Capua (about a hundred miles south of Rome) escaped and began terrorizing the surrounding countryside. They were led by a man named Spartacus, who had the foresight to realize that gladiators were, one-on-one, a match for Roman soldiers. Under his command, the escapees trained a number of runaway slaves to fight and proceeded to defeat two small Roman armies the Senate sent against them.

The senators had been certain that the forces they had dispatched would be more than adequate. After all, most free Romans, especially members of the aristocratic class, viewed slaves and gladiators as almost less than human and certainly no match for Roman soldiers in a fight. Shocked by the success of the rebels, the senators now worried that the crisis might escalate into a full-scale uprising involving millions of slaves, which would threaten Rome's very existence. Clearly, it was time to send in the first-string commanders and troops. In Plutarch's words:

There was now more to disturb the Senate than just the shame and disgrace of the revolt. The situation had become dangerous enough to inspire real fear, and as a result both consuls were sent out to deal with what was considered a major war and a most difficult one to fight.[22]

Once again, the senators had underestimated the enemy. Spartacus and his army, which now numbered in the tens of thousands, crushed the forces of the consul C. Lentulus Clodianus. Appalled and now desperate, the Senate appointed a wealthy and influential financier (actually the richest man in Rome), Marcus Licinius Crassus, to put down the insurrection. At first, Crassus's campaign did not go as well as he and his senatorial backers had hoped it would. So the senators recalled the noted general Gnaeus Pompeius (popularly known as Pompey) from a military command in Spain to aid Crassus. This was upsetting for Crassus, who did not want to share the glory for defeating the slaves with a rival commander. As Plutarch said, Crassus correctly predicted "that the credit for the success would be likely to go not to himself but to the commander who appeared on the scene with reinforcements."[23]

To forestall such an event, Crassus launched an immediate attack on Spartacus, which was successful. Nevertheless, the victor's worst fear came to pass when Pompey arrived just in time to capture several thousand of the retreating slaves and take most of the credit for the victory. The Senate even granted Pompey the honor of the victory parade, much to Crassus's displeasure.

THE SENATE VERSUS CAESAR

The actions of the senators during the first-century-B.C. slave uprising clearly illustrate the important role they played in maintaining domestic security. Not only did they supply the funds to support the troops, they also sent armies and consuls into the field, appointed a special commander (Crassus), transferred a general (Pompey) from overseas, and granted the triumph after the final victory. This was, by modern standards, an extraordinary display of military power by a group of legislators. In contrast, although the U.S. Senate can (in concert with the House of Representatives) declare and fund a war, it cannot assign the generals and decide military strategy.

Of course, the true test of the Senate's national security powers was whether it was successful in using them. In the long run, the senators' policies and efforts worked against Hannibal, Spartacus, and a number of other threats against the homeland. But the Senate finally met its match when a major portion of the very army it employed to achieve internal security turned on it, initiating disastrous civil war.

This crisis began in 58 B.C. when a former consul, and a senator himself, Julius Caesar, took charge of the provinces of Cisalpine Gaul (encompassing northern Italy) and Narbonese Gaul (southern France). Caesar spent several years subduing the natives of what are now central and northern France, actions sanctioned by the Senate. But in the process, he created a large, battle-hardened army that was more loyal to him than to the state. Back in Rome, the Senate, the consuls, and Pompey (by then the Senate's number one general) now viewed Caesar as a serious potential threat.

In an attempt to remove that threat, the Senate ordered Caesar to lay down command of his army. But he refused. So the senators relieved him of his governorship. Undaunted, the ambitious Caesar responded by defying the Senate and marching on Rome. Pompey and many of the senators fled and years of civil strife ensued, at the end of which the Republic lay in ruins and the Senate was nearly powerless. In a twist of fate no one had foreseen, the great security and military power of the Senate had become the instrument of its undoing.

CHAPTER 3

THE SENATE AND FOREIGN RELATIONS

The Senate's handling of the invasion of Hannibal in the third century B.C. can be seen foremost as an example of that august body of upper-class Romans working to maintain domestic security. Yet Hannibal's attack on the Roman heartland was also part of Rome's larger war with Carthage, a foreign nation; so in dealing with the overall threat, the Senate exercised not only its domestic security powers but also its nearly supreme authority in Roman foreign affairs. According to Polybius, the senators were

> responsible for dispatching embassies or commissions to countries outside Italy, either to settle differences, to offer advice, to impose demands, to receive submissions [surrenders], or to declare war. And in the same way, whenever any foreign delegations arrive in Rome, it [the Senate] decides how they should be received, and what answer should be given to them.[24]

One section of this passage by Polybius is a generalization and can be somewhat misleading. Technically speaking, the republican constitution vested the authority to declare war in the people, who voted for or against it in one of the popular assemblies, the *comitum centuriata*. Still, the senators were almost always able to overshadow, sway, or manipulate the war decisions of that assembly. This was partly because the senators were the first people in Italy to receive information about foreign events and were privy to details of foreign negotiations, ultimatums, and treaties that the voters were not. Indeed, more often than not, the voters in the assembly knew only as much about a foreign crisis or event as the senators wanted them to know.

F.R. Cowell adds that "the senators debated upon terms of peace before they were submitted to the people for ratification." These and other factors usually ensured that the Senate had more practical control over declaring war and making peace than either the people or the generals. "Woe betide a Roman commander," says Cowell, "who accepted conditions of peace that the Senate did not like! More than one such unfortunate man was sent back to his enemies in chains with a disavowal of his treaty."[25]

ULTIMATUM AND WAR DECLARATION

A classic example of the Roman Senate exercising its authority in several aspects of foreign relations, including making war and peace, was the manner in which the senators handled the Second Punic War, in which Hannibal ended up invading Italy. The Romans had earlier defeated the Carthaginians in the First Punic War (262–241 B.C.). And in the years following that conflict, Hannibal's father, Hamilcar Barca, had built up a formidable power base in Spain. The Romans watched this warily. They had an ally there—the city of Saguntum, on the eastern coast—

The Roman people usually learned about foreign events through government spokesmen.

which seemed threatened by the Carthaginian presence in the region. And the Senate grew increasingly uneasy about the buildup of Carthaginian troops on European soil. (Carthage had once controlled most of the island of Sicily, which was part of Europe, but had been driven out during the first war with Rome.)

Eventually, following Hamilcar's death, Hannibal took charge of Carthage's operations in Spain, and it soon appeared that he might move against Saguntum. Naturally fearful, the Saguntines sent ambassadors to the Senate in Rome. The ambassadors informed the senators of Hannibal's war preparations and beseeched them to abide by their alliance and send help if it was needed. The Senate accordingly sent a group of commissioners, including several senators, to Spain to investigate the situation. These men managed to arrange a meeting with Hannibal himself. According to Polybius, they demanded that he "leave Saguntum alone, which they claimed lay within their sphere of influence, and to refrain from crossing the Ebro [River, several miles north of Saguntum]." Hannibal responded with hostility to the senators and their demands. "In his dealings with the Romans," Polybius writes,

he was in a mood of unreasoning and violent anger, and so did not cite . . . the real cause of his country's grievances. . . . He gave the impression that he was embarking on the war not only in defiance of reason, but even of justice.[26]

The senators had delivered their ultimatum to Hannibal and he had rebuffed it. Concluding that war was probably inevitable, the delegates departed Spain and sailed for Carthage to deliver the same ultimatum to the Carthaginian government. Not long afterward, however, Hannibal attacked Saguntum, as the Saguntines and Romans had feared he would. This forced the members of the Senate in Rome into a debate over going to war. As Livy tells it:

The Senate met to reconsider the situation. Opinions were divided. Some [senators] proposed that . . . total war, by sea and land, should be undertaken; others preferred to concentrate wholly against Hannibal in Spain. [A third group of senators] expressed the view that it would be wiser to await the return of the envoys . . . as so serious a step as war with Carthage ought not to be taken without full deliberation. It was this last, and most cautious, proposal which was adopted.[27]

The Senate soon decided that, with the siege of Saguntum ongoing, it could not waste too much precious

❧ AN EARLY SENATORIAL TREATY ❧

The Senate and people of Rome negotiated three separate treaties with Carthage in the centuries preceding the Punic Wars. In his Histories, *Polybius summarizes their provisions. The following excerpts are from the second treaty, the exact date of which Polybius did not know, but was almost surely sometime in the fourth century* B.C.

There shall be friendship on the following conditions between the Romans and their allies, and the Carthaginians . . . and their respective allies. The Romans shall not make raids, or trade or found a city on the farther side of the Fair Promontory, Mastia, or Tarsium [the locations of which are now unknown]. . . . If any Carthaginians take prisoner any of a people with whom the Romans have a treaty of peace in writing . . . they shall not bring them into Roman harbors. . . . The Romans shall not do likewise. If a Roman obtains water and provisions from any place which is under Carthaginian rule, he shall not use these supplies to do harm to any member of a people with whom the Carthaginians enjoy peace and friendship. Neither shall a Carthaginian act in this way.

time. So it dispatched a group of negotiators to Carthage to demand that the Carthaginian government disavow its allegiance to Hannibal and turn him over to Rome. The senators who confronted the Carthaginian leaders listened to a spokesman explain why Carthage had every right to pursue its present policies in Spain. But as Polybius recorded, the Roman envoys had no intention of debating the situation with the enemy:

After they had heard the Carthaginians' statement of their case, [the senators] spoke no word in reply, but the senior member of the delegation pointed to the bosom of his toga and declared to the [Carthaginian leaders] that in its folds he carried both peace and war, and that he would let fall from it whichever they had instructed him to leave. The Carthaginians . . . [angrily] answered that he should bring out whichever he thought best, and when the envoy replied that it would be war, many of the [Carthaginians] shouted at once, "We accept it!" It was on these terms that the Senate and the Roman ambassadors departed.[28]

When news of these events reached Rome, the senators informed the assembly that Carthage would not halt its attack on Saguntum. Negotiations had failed, former treaties with Carthage had been broken, Rome's honor had been challenged, and war was inevitable. Hearing the senators make such a strong case for war, the voters in the assembly did what was expected of them and passed the war declaration.

THE SENATE MAKES PEACE
This brief summary of the Senate in action in the early days of the Second Punic War demonstrates some of the ways that it undertook foreign negotiations. The manner in which the senators negotiated the Carthaginian surrender and peace treaty at the conclusion of the same war is also revealing. Fortunately, both Livy and Polybius covered the conflict and its immediate aftermath in considerable detail. Their writings tell how the Ro-

A Roman envoy (raising part of his toga at right) warns Carthaginian leaders that they may face a second war with Rome.

mans rebounded after their severe initial losses to Hannibal. Unable to bring the Romans to their knees, Hannibal and his soldiers roamed through Italy for several years, with Roman forces constantly harassing and containing them. Finally, the Romans opened up a major new war front by crossing to North Africa and attacking the Carthaginian heartland. Hannibal had to return to Africa to defend his country. There, on the plain of Zama, not far from Carthage, he experienced the first and only military defeat of his illustrious career.

At this point, Carthage had no other choice but surrender, and the stage was set for the Roman Senate to negotiate the terms. Envoys from Carthage arrived in Rome early in 201 B.C. and stood before the senators, who for symbolic purposes met in the temple of the Roman war goddess Bellona. (She was often portrayed as the wife of Mars, and artistic renderings show her riding a war chariot and brandishing a sword and flaming torch.) These Carthaginians had to endure a patriotic speech by one of the senators, who, according to Livy,

> described the battle [of Zama], the last one the Carthaginians would ever fight, and the end which had come at last to [the Romans'] sufferings in the war. . . . [Next he addressed] the [crowds of] people [who had gathered] outside so that

all could share in the general rejoicing. Then all the temples throughout the city were opened for offering thanks, and three days of public thanksgiving were decreed [by the Senate]. . . . The Senate then turned its attention to the [Carthaginian] envoys . . . [who] were indisputably the leading citizens of their country. [They admitted that Rome was invincible and] recounted the former great wealth of Carthage and the depths to which she had fallen. . . . [They pleaded that] their city and ancestral homes would remain theirs only if the Roman people were willing to withhold its fury and spare them the worst fate of all.

Having subjected the Carthaginian negotiators to this round of ritual humiliations, "the entire Senate was now prepared to make peace."[29]

The first major step the senators took in concluding the peace, in keeping with the legal procedures of the constitution, was to go to the people's assembly and get a formal vote authorizing it. Some of the senators urged the assembly to appoint Publius Cornelius Scipio, who had defeated Hannibal at Zama and was also a senator, to negotiate the treaty. Next, the senators dealt with the issue of the hundreds of Carthaginian citizens who were being held in Roman jails. According to Livy, the Carthaginian envoys

Publius Cornelius Scipio received the title "Africanus" after defeating Hannibal at Zama in North Africa. Scipio negotiated the treaty that ended the conflict.

begged permission [from the Senate] . . . to speak to their fellow citizens. . . . When this was granted, they made the further request that they should be given the opportunity of ransoming certain chosen prisoners; and on request [they] furnished some two hundred names. The Senate passed a decree that [the prisoners should be restored] to their own people without ransom if an agreement was reached about terms of peace.[30]

THE TREATY: ACCEPT OR REJECT?

When the Carthaginian envoys returned to Carthage, they met with Scipio, who had received his orders from the Senate about drawing up the treaty, which was not negotiable. Scipio first set forth those terms that were essentially concessions made by the Romans out of a spirit of mercy and goodwill. The Roman Senate and people, he said, would allow Carthage to retain all of its cities, farmland, livestock, and slaves. Furthermore, the Carthaginians would be allowed to continue governing themselves under their own laws. And no Roman soldiers would be garrisoned in Carthage as an occupation force.

The rest of the terms of the treaty were not nearly as generous and lenient. Following the guidelines approved by his fellow senators, Scipio

announced that Carthage must pay large war reparations (money and/or other valuables to cover the damages the Carthaginians had caused to Rome's people and property). Also, as Polybius recorded:

All their [battle] elephants and all ships of war, with the exception of ten [ships], were to be surrendered. They [the Carthaginians] were not to make war on any people outside Africa at all, and on none in Africa without consent from Rome. . . . They were to provide the Roman army with sufficient corn for three months and with pay until a reply should be received from Rome concerning the treaty. . . . And they were to hand over as a guarantee of good faith 100 hostages. These were to be chosen by the Roman commander from among the young men of the country between the ages of fourteen and thirty.[31]

When these terms set forth by Scipio in the name of the Roman Senate were presented to the Carthaginian legislature (which resembled the Roman Senate in some ways), at first many of the legislators balked. Evidently they considered the terms too harsh, which in truth they were not when one considers the huge extent of Rome's losses in the war. One of the Carthaginians actually mounted the

☙ HANNIBAL ENDORSES ❧ THE SENATE'S TREATY

According to Polybius in his Histories, *this is the complete speech Hannibal gave to the Carthaginian legislature as he urged them to accept the terms of the treaty imposed by the Roman Senate.*

It seems to me amazing, and indeed quite beyond my comprehension, that anyone who is a citizen of Carthage and has full knowledge of the policies which we have both individually and collectively adopted against Rome should not thank his stars that now that we are at their mercy we have obtained such lenient terms [from the Roman Senate]. If you had been asked only a few days ago what you expected your country would suffer in the event of a Roman victory, the disasters which threatened us then appeared so overwhelming that you would not even have been able to express your fears. So now I beg you not even to debate the question, but to declare your acceptance of the proposals unanimously, to offer up sacrifices to the gods, and to pray with one voice the Roman [Senate] and people may ratify the treaty!

speaker's platform and began to denounce the treaty, despite the fact that Roman observers were in the room. At this point, according to Polybius, none other than Hannibal himself "came forward and forcibly pulled [the speaker] down from the platform." When the other legislators objected to this violent gesture, Hannibal

> appealed to them not to confine their attention to the question of whether he had violated the procedure of the house; they should rather consider whether or not he was genuinely concerned for his country. . . . "It seems to me amazing," he told them . . . "that any-

one who is a citizen of Carthage and has full knowledge of the policies which we have . . . adopted against Rome should not thank his stars that now that we are at their mercy we have obtained such lenient terms [from the Roman Senate]. . . . I beg you not even to debate the question, but to declare your acceptance of the proposals unanimously . . . and to pray with one voice the Roman [Senate] and people may ratify the treaty!"[32]

Hearing the wisdom of Hannibal's words, his fellow Carthaginian leaders accepted the terms of the treaty. And when news of this acceptance reached Rome, the senators gave their own approval and dutifully acquired the rubber stamp of the assembly. In this way, the Senate and its representatives concluded an honorable peace to a seventeen-year-long conflict (the largest in world history up to that time) that had wiped out almost an entire generation of Roman men.

FOREIGN POLICY MISTAKES

Declaring war and making peace treaties were only two aspects of the work the Roman senators accom-plished in the realm of foreign policy during the Republic. The Senate was also in charge of sending envoys, ambassadors, and commissioners to foreign lands. These men, who were often senators themselves, sometimes had the task of concluding alliances with the leaders of these lands. Or the senators might offer such leaders advice or help them settle disputes with their neighbors, especially if such settlements were in Rome's interest.

Conversely, the Senate sometimes tried to provoke quarrels between

After suffering a series of defeats by the Romans and a rebellion by his own son, Mithradates VI, king of Pontus (at right), committed suicide.

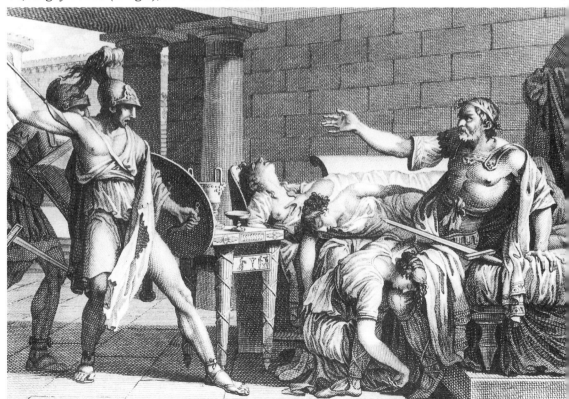

foreign states—again, when it seemed to be in Rome's interest. This approach sometimes had beneficial results. But other times it ended up causing more harm than good, as exemplified by an incident that occurred in 91–90 B.C. About twenty-five years before, trouble had begun to brew in the small kingdom of Northern Cappadocia, situated in northern Asia Minor (what is now Turkey) on the southern shore of the Black Sea. At age eighteen, Mithradates, a prince of the local royal family, usurped the throne from his brother (and mother, who was serving as regent for the two young men). Hugely ambitious, Mithradates built up a formidable army and used it to extend his power westward to the Danube River; this created a new and larger kingdom called Pontus.

Eventually, Mithradates' expansionist policies placed him on a collision course with Rome. Roman settlers were multiplying in the recently established Roman province of Asia, making up the western third of Asia Minor, directly south of Pontus and its small neighbor, Bithynia. Mithradates grew bold and occupied Bithynia. Hearing of this move, the Senate sent envoys, who warned him to withdraw or face the consequences. Unprepared for all-out war with the most powerful nation on earth, Mithradates relented and withdrew.

Not content with this modest success, the senators proceeded with a covert policy designed to weaken Pontus using a third party, namely Bithynia. In the winter of 91–90 B.C., the Senate secretly encouraged the king of Bithynia to send raiding parties into Pontus. But this policy soon backfired. In making foreign policy decisions, the senators were always crucially dependent on intelligence, that is, information gathered by various Roman representatives and spies stationed in other lands. In this case, the Senate's intelligence was unreliable because it overestimated the strength of the Bithynian ruler and grossly underestimated Mithradates' strength. In 89 B.C., the latter suddenly invaded and overran both Bithynia and the nearby Roman province. Some eighty thousand Roman settlers and merchants were slaughtered. (Fortunately for Rome, the Senate was able to rectify its mistake by sending generals and troops, who eventually defeated Mithradates.)

Successful Use of Intimidation

In contrast, sometimes the Senate's forceful foreign policy moves were successful and achieved the desired results. One of the most famous examples was the so-called Circle of Popilius. In the early second century B.C., the Romans invaded various Greek-ruled lands in the eastern Mediterranean sphere, including the kingdom of Macedonia. Two rival

An engraving shows Gaius Popilius Laenas drawing a circle around King Antiochus IV. This blatant tactic of intimidation had the desired effect.

Greek kingdoms—Seleucia (encompassing Syria and other parts of the Near East) and Egypt (ruled by the descendants of the Greek military general Ptolemy)—were affected by or tried to take advantage of the ongoing changes in the region's balance of power. During the Roman-Macedonian conflict, for instance, Antiochus IV, king of Seleucia, invaded Egypt.

The Senate reasoned that if Seleucia extended its sway into Africa and grew stronger and richer, it would eventually prove a threat to Rome's domination of the Mediterranean. So the senators sent Gaius Popilius Laenas to Egypt. Popilius and his entourage found Antiochus near the capital city of Alexandria (on Egypt's northern coast). In Livy's words, as the Romans approached,

the king greeted them and stretched out his right hand to Popilius. Whereupon, Popilius handed him the tablets containing the Senate's resolution [stating that Antiochus must vacate Egypt] in writing and bade him read this before doing anything else. After reading the decree, Antiochus said that he would summon his friends and consult with them about his course of action; at which Popilius . . . drew a circle round the king with the rod he carried in his hand

and said: "Before you move out of this circle, give me an answer to report to the Senate." The king hesitated for a moment, astounded by the violence of the command, then replied, "I shall do what the Senate decrees." Not until then did Popilius hold out his hand to the king as an ally and friend. Antiochus then withdrew from Egypt by the appointed day.[33]

TREMENDOUS POWER IN WORLD AFFAIRS

Another stark example of the Senate's ability to change the international balance of power occurred not long after the incident with Popilius and Antiochus. Ever since their defeat in 201 B.C., the Carthaginians had faithfully honored the terms of the peace treaty the Senate had forced them to ratify. They had paid the heavy war repara-

---

⚜ CATO AND THE FIGS ⚜

In his biography of Cato the Censor (translated by Ian Scott-Kilvert in Makers of Rome*), Plutarch tells how the crusty old senator emphasized his contempt for Carthage by ending every speech with the words, "Carthage must be destroyed!" Another tactic Cato used, according to Plutarch, involved Carthaginian fruit.*

to drop some Libyan [North African] figs on the floor of the Senate House, and when the senators admired their size and beauty, he remarked that the country which produced them [i.e., Carthage] was only three days' sail from Rome.

[Cato] warned the Senate that the overwhelming defeats and misfortunes which the Carthaginians had suffered had done . . . little to impair their strength, and that they were likely to emerge not weaker but more experienced in war. . . . As he ended this speech, it is said that Cato shook the folds of his toga and contrived

Cato the Elder shows his fellow senators some North African figs to emphasize Carthage's prosperity.

tions demanded in the treaty and refrained from either building a new war fleet or getting involved in foreign conflicts.

However, a number of Romans, especially some who had fought or lost relatives in the Second Punic War, were not satisfied with this situation. They wanted to see Carthage suffer harsher punishment. The most influential member of these "Carthage haters" was Marcus Porcius Cato (born 234 B.C.), also known as "Cato the Censor" because of the strict moral rules he enforced when serving in that public office. He was also one of the most accomplished and influential senators Rome ever produced.

In 153 B.C., when he was in his eighties, Cato paid a visit to Carthage as part of a senatorial commission. He was both surprised and disturbed to see the city and its people enjoying unbridled prosperity and happiness. Cato knew only too well how many Roman families had suffered, and were still suffering, from their losses in the great war. And the fact that he saw no overt suffering in Carthage made him seethe with anger. He also convinced himself that sooner or later the Carthaginians would once again become warlike and pose a threat to his own nation. According to Plutarch: "He found Carthage teeming with a new genera-

tion of fighting men, overflowing with wealth, amply stocked with weapons and military supplies of every kind, and full of confidence at this revival of its strength."[34]

For these reasons, the bitter old senator dedicated himself to bringing about Carthage's downfall. When he returned to Rome, he began lobbying for a third Punic war that would, he hoped, rid the world of Carthage once and for all. Thereafter, Cato ended every speech he made in the Senate, no matter what the topic, with the words *"Delenda est Carthago!"* ("Carthage must be destroyed!"). He got his wish. He steadily won over his fellow senators, who found excuses to declare war on Carthage for a third time. Cato did not live long enough to see the destruction his hatred and perseverance brought about because he died in 149 B.C., the very year that Rome launched operations against Carthage. Although the Carthaginians staged a desperate and heroic resistance, their fate was sealed. Three years later, the Romans almost completely destroyed the city and either killed or enslaved all of its inhabitants. This series of events demonstrated perhaps more emphatically than any other the tremendous power in world affairs wielded by a small handful of Roman senators in the later years of the Republic.

CHAPTER 4

SENATORIAL MEETINGS, SPEECHES, AND DECREES

Numerous stories describing the decrees and actions taken by the Roman Senate in domestic and foreign affairs have survived in the writings of Livy, Polybius, Plutarch, Cicero, and other ancient writers. These actions range from declaring war and making peace treaties to directing the strategy of military generals and controlling the state purse. Unfortunately, however, very little information has survived about the actual daily work of the senators. Detailed official records were kept of every meeting of the Senate, just as minutes are kept of every meeting of the U.S. Senate today, but none of these ancient records have survived. So the actual rules of order that guided the senators' seating plans, order of speeches and debate, voting procedures, seniority privileges, and so on are now only sketchy at best. And the manner in which the Senate physically convened and did its business must be tentatively pieced together from scattered clues in the surviving works of ancient writers.

THE SENATE HOUSE

On the plus side, the main meeting place of the Senate is one of the best preserved of all ancient Roman buildings. Technically speaking, Roman law allowed the senators to convene their meetings anywhere within a radius of one mile of the city of Rome. And they sometimes gathered in temples, courthouses, and other places. Most of the time, however, meetings of the Senate took place in the Senate House, or Curia Hostilia (often more simply called the Curia). It was located in the northwest corner of Rome's main public square, the Forum Romanum.

The original Curia was erected in the sixth century B.C. by Tullus Hostilius, the legendary third king of Rome. Presumably this was where the senators, then advisers to the monarch, met to discuss affairs of state. The building underwent frequent repairs over the years, until it was destroyed in a fire in 52 B.C. A new building replaced it. But shortly afterward, Julius Caesar, who had declared himself dictator for life and whose own powers now overshadowed those of the senators, decided to build another Senate House. Thus, the recently restored structure was dismantled to make way for new construction projects and Caesar ordered work to begin on his own Curia. It was completed in 29 B.C., fifteen years after Caesar's assassination. The new structure weathered the early years of the Empire, undergoing various repairs until the emperor Domitian restored it in the 80s A.D. Almost exactly two centuries later, in 283, fire claimed the Senate House again. This time the emperor Diocletian rebuilt it; this is the version that still stands in the ruined Forum today.

As near as scholars can tell, the building erected by Diocletian reused the foundation of its predecessor and closely resembled the earlier structure. (This is not surprising. The Romans

The Curia as it appears today, one of the best-preserved structures in the Roman Forum.

were sticklers about maintaining tradition and for most of their history were reluctant to alter the architectural, artistic, clothing, and other styles of their ancestors.) Therefore, it is likely that the Curia standing today is not much different from the one in which Caesar and the great Cicero once stood and delivered their renowned speeches. It is rectangular, with a simple pitched roof, and measures about seventy-five by eighty-five feet.

Walking into the building, one is immediately struck by the beauty of the floor. Composed of fine Numidian and Phrygian marble, its design features alternating squares and rectangles containing green and red rosettes set against yellow and purple backgrounds. The walls are now plain and stark. But in ancient times the brick

This reconstruction of the interior of the Senate House for a movie shows some of the senators standing behind more senior seated members.

❧ CICERO CRITICIZES OTHER ORATORS ❧

In his biography of Cicero (translated by Rex Warner in Fall of the Roman Republic*), Plutarch describes the great senator's critique of other orators who spoke in the Senate and law courts.*

In the case of Cicero, elocution and delivery were an important element in his powers of persuasion. He used to ridicule those who were given to shouting out their speeches and said that, just as lame men rode on horseback because they could not walk, so these orators shouted because they could not speak. This ready wit and jesting habit of his was regarded as a good and attractive quality in a lawyer [and in a senator].

façade was covered by a veneer of marble extending from the floor to a point two-thirds of the distance to the ceiling. The upper third of the walls contained painted mosaics, and the ceiling was richly decorated with carved designs, perhaps gilded in gold leaf.

The question most often asked by modern visitors to the surviving Curia is, Where did the senators sit? The answer is revealed by the presence of three broad step-levels that rise on either side of the central floor space. The senators' chairs originally rested on these levels, and it appears that there was room for about three hundred chairs. It is clear, therefore, that the building (and the earlier versions that it replicates) could accommodate the standard number of senators throughout most of the republican years—three hundred.

In 80 B.C., however, the number of senators increased to six hundred. And Julius Caesar added another three hundred, for a total of nine hundred. (Augustus, the first emperor, reduced the number of senators to six hundred, but in the later years of the Empire, the number soared to as high as two thousand.) Where did all these extra senators sit during the late Republic and the Empire? No one knows for sure. But it seems probable that they did not all sit; rather, senior members were entitled to the chairs and the rest likely stood behind them. Thus, when it was in use, this relatively small building must have been quite crowded from Caesar's time onward.

A SENATORIAL MEETING COMES TO ORDER

As for what a meeting of these gathered senators was like, what follows is a likely scenario pieced together from remarks made in various ancient works. First, law required that meetings be called by a consul, a praetor, or, after 287 B.C., a tribune. At the appointed time, the senators filed in to the Curia (or temple or other building if the meeting was held elsewhere). No non-senators were allowed to attend, with the exception of the sons and grandsons of senators, presumably so that they could learn how affairs of state worked. These young men could stand and watch, provided they remained still and quiet.

Once everyone had gathered, a priest conducted a sacrifice out of respect for and to obtain the favor of the gods. This consisted of sprinkling water over the sacrificial animal (called the victim) to purify it symbolically and then cutting its throat and letting the blood flow out into a bowl. (Because of the confined space, the victims were likely small animals such as pigs and goats; larger beasts, especially cattle, were sacrificed in larger ceremonies held at outdoor altars on the steps or grounds of temples.)

Following the sacrifice, a high official, usually one of the consuls (who were more often than not also senators), called the meeting to order and presided. First, he announced the nature of the day's business, that is, the reason or reasons why the meeting had been called. Then he began asking the senators for their opinions.

(The official could not take part in the debate, nor could he vote on resolutions and decrees; he was strictly a moderator.) It seems that he had to follow a set pecking order based on seniority. By tradition, the oldest and most experienced senator, known as the *Princeps Senatus*, spoke first, followed by the next-most experienced senator, and so forth.

Another pecking order that may have been used at one time or another was based on the importance of the prior public offices held by the various senators. In such a scheme, ex-consuls and ex-censors spoke first because consuls and censors were the most powerful and prestigious of the magistrates. Their comments were followed by those of ex-praetors, ex-aediles, and so on.

PREPARING AND DELIVERING SPEECHES

A lively debate might ensue, which sometimes included speeches made by various senators. It is possible that some senators delivered their speeches, especially if they were fairly short, from their chairs; perhaps they stood up so that everyone in the room could better see and hear them. Many of the speeches in the U.S. Senate and British Parliament are given in this manner. It appears that longer, more important, and prepared speeches were delivered in the open floor space in the center of the main chamber of the Curia.

A senator makes an impassioned plea during a meeting of the Senate. The ability to speak persuasively was essential to Roman statesmen.

All of the senators were trained to give speeches and were used to giving them. After all, they were all ex-magistrates who could not have attained and conducted their high offices without making frequent speeches to the people. Public speaking was the main form of mass communication in ancient Rome, and a large portion of a well-to-do young man's education was devoted to learning the art of rhetoric. Speeches in the Senate could take many forms, depending on their length and purpose. But in the case of long, prepared speeches, it was most common for senators to follow most or all of the five basic elements of formal rhetoric.

The first of these five elements, *inventio*, or "invention," consisted of research, that is, finding the proper materials—facts, names, anecdotes, and so on—to support the main point or argument of the speech. In the second element of rhetoric, *collocatio*, or "arrangement," the senator arranged the materials in an ordered, logical, and effective manner. In the third element, *elocutio*, or "diction," he chose the most effective tone of voice and manner of delivery (which might be loud and forceful, quiet and subdued, or something in between). In *memoria*, or "memory," he memorized the speech. And finally, in *actio*, his "delivery," he utilized a wide array of vocal techniques and physical gestures to make the speech more effective.

In a very real way, major public speeches in the Senate were performances designed to move an audience. And in this respect, mastering *elocutio* and *actio*, which determined the effectiveness of the speaker's delivery, was essential to any senator who desired to be influential. Cicero recognizes this in the following passage from one of his works about oratory:

A leading speaker will vary and modulate his voice, raising and lowering it and deploying the full scale of tones. He will avoid extravagant gestures and stand impressively erect. He will not pace about and when he does so, not for any distance. He should not dart forward except in moderation with strict control. There should be no effeminate [womanly] bending of the neck or twiddling of his fingers or beating out the rhythm of his cadences on his knuckles. He should control himself by the way he holds and moves his entire body. He should extend his arm at

moments of high dispute and lower it during calmer passages. . . . Once he has made sure he does not have a stupid expression on his face and/or a grimace, he should control his eyes with great care, for as the face is the image of the soul, the eyes are its translators. Depending on the subject at hand, they can express grief or hilarity.[35]

SENATORIAL DECREES

The speeches given by the senators sometimes lasted for only a few hours. But they might take all day or even two or more days. Eventually, after all opinions had been aired, one or more members called for some kind of action to be taken. If the subject of debate was an impending law to be voted on by the popular assembly, one or more senators took on the task of preparing the legislation, or perhaps amending an existing bill, and submitting it to the assembly.

When appropriate, the senators also drafted resolutions, proclamations, and decrees. Known collectively as *decreta* or *senatus consulta*, these were technically not laws because they were not passed by the assembly, the official law-making body of the state. However, because of the traditional dignity and prestige of the Senate, the magistrates and people usually accepted and treated a *senatus consultum* as if it were a law. This un-

❧ NERVOUS BEFORE A SPEECH ☙

Even Cicero, one of the greatest senators and orators Rome ever produced, got nervous before delivering a speech before a packed Senate chamber or courtroom, as he admits in this passage from his speech For Cluentius *(translated by Michael Grant in* Cicero: Murder Trials*).*

[When] I rose to [speak] . . . I was filled with anxiety, uneasiness, apprehension. I am always very nervous when I begin a speech. Every time I get up to speak I feel like it is I myself who am on trial, not merely for my competence but for my integrity and conscience as well. I fluctuate between two fears. Either I shall be claiming more than I can achieve, which would be impudent, or I shall not be making the best of my case, which would be a blameworthy act of negligence, a failure to meet my obligations.

derscores the tremendous legal authority of the Senate despite the fact that it was not actually a law-making body. Robert Byrd provides more specific information about these senatorial resolutions:

The *senatus consultum* contained the name of the presiding magistrate, the date, the place of assembly [where the Senate was meeting], and the terms or substance of the *senatus consultum.* It indicated the number of senators who were present when the [decree] was approved. It also gave the names of witnesses to the drafting of the *senatus consultum*, and it included the capital letter "C," indicating that the Senate had given its approval.[36]

These formal elements of decrees can be seen in a surviving example—the *senatus consultum* that banned the rites of Bacchus in 186 B.C., which states in part:

Quintus Marcius . . . and Spurius Potumius . . . consuls for that year, consulted the Senate on October 7 in the temple of Bellona. Marcus Claudius . . . Lucius Valerius . . . and Quintus Minucius . . . were witnesses to the recording of this decree. With reference to Bacchanalia, the senators advised . . . the following. . . . "Let no one of them plan to hold Bacchanalia in his home. . . . Let no man be a priest [of Bacchus]. Let no man or woman be a deacon. . . . Let no one plan to hold cult ceremonies in public or in private or outside the city unless [it is] . . . in accordance with the recommendations of the Senate."[37]

Catiline (at lower right) sits shunned by his fellow senators, as Cicero exposes his plot to overthrow the government.

The 186 B.C. senatorial decree was only one of many that was accepted as legally binding by the Roman people. In contrast, occasionally public opinion was squarely against the content of a senatorial decree. In such a case, the constitution provided a method of redress: A tribune could use his veto power to nullify the resolution.

THE SENATE'S "LAST DECREE"

Another kind of decree the Senate issued, though far less frequently, was the *senatus consultum ultimum* (literally the "final resolution of the Senate"),

often referred to simply as the "last decree." It was designed to deal with serious threats to the security of the state in a national emergency. The last decree authorized the consuls and other chief magistrates to use any means necessary to protect the republican state. These included suspending people's rights of legal appeal, declaring martial law, and even applying military force.

The *senatus consultum ultimum* was first used in 121 B.C. and the senators issued it only nine more times between that date and 49 B.C. Between 49 and 40 B.C., a period in which the Republic was wracked by civil war and political turmoil, the last decree was invoked about five times. On January 7, 49 B.C., for example, the senators passed it in a last-ditch attempt to reduce the power of Julius Caesar, whose army was poised to march on Rome. In this case, the last decree was ineffective. Instead of confronting and disarming Caesar, many of the magistrates, joined by hundreds of senators, fled and he entered Rome largely unopposed.

Perhaps the most famous example of the passage of the *senatus consultum ultimum*, one in which it *was* effective, occurred in 63 B.C. This incident is particularly notable for revealing some of the actual work of the senators, including their reaction to a crisis and the manner and content of their speeches. The events leading to the emergency in question were as follows. Lucius Sergius Catilina, popularly known as Catiline, was a debt-ridden nobleman of questionable integrity. In 64 B.C., hoping to shore up his bad reputation, he entered the consular elections, which chose the consuls for the following year. But he was up against the formidable Cicero, who won, along with another popular leader named Antonius. In 63 (the year Cicero and Antonius served their terms), Catiline ran for consul again and lost again.

Furious and resentful, Catiline now plotted revenge. He planned to murder the consuls and seize control of the government. But he and his ragtag band of followers were not careful enough, and word of what they were up to leaked out and reached the leading magistrates, including Cicero. The Roman historian Sallust, who was in Rome at the time, tells how Cicero got the Senate to issue the *senatus consultum ultimum:*

> The news of these events greatly disturbed Cicero. . . . The city could no longer be protected from the conspirators by unofficial action on his part. . . . He therefore apprised the Senate of the matter. . . . In accordance with its usual practice in serious emergencies, the Senate decreed that the consuls "should take measures for the defense of the realm," thus conferring upon them the most extensive powers that Roman custom allows it to entrust to magistrates [i.e., the last decree]. This decree authorizes them to levy troops and conduct war, to apply unlimited force to allies and citizens alike, and to exercise supreme command and jurisdiction both at home and abroad.[38]

SETTING A BAD PRECEDENT

The manner in which Cicero exposed Catiline to the Senate was highly dramatic—a series of speeches that were among the most memorable in that body's history. For the first speech, Catiline, who was then himself a senator, was actually sitting in the main chamber of the Senate House when Cicero walked to the center of the room and said:

In the name of heaven, Catilina, how long will you exploit our patience? Surely your insane activities cannot escape our retaliation forever! Are there to be no limits to this swaggering, ungovernable recklessness? The garrison which guards the Palatine [Hill] by night, the patrols ranging the city, the terror that grips the population, the amassing of all loyal citizens on one single spot, this meeting of the Senate behind strongly fortified defenses, the expressions on the countenances of each man here— have none of these sights made the slightest impact on your heart? You must be well aware that your plot has been detected. Now that every single person in this place knows all about your conspiracy, you cannot fail to realize it is doomed. . . . What a scandalous commentary on our age and its standards! For the Senate knows all about these things. The consul sees them being done. And yet this man [Catiline] still lives! Lives? He

---

◈ THE SENATE DEBATES LIFE OR DEATH ◈

In this excerpt from his fourth speech against Catiline (translated by Michael Grant in Selected Political Speeches of Cicero*), Cicero sums up the two sides of the debate in the Senate about what should be done with the captured Catilinian conspirators who had been planning to overthrow the government.*

I see that up to now there are two proposals. One was made by Decimus Silanus [a recently elected consul], who moved that the men who have attempted to destroy our community should be put to death. The other is the proposal of Julius Caesar, who sets aside the death penalty but welcomes the full rigor of all the other punishments. . . . Silanus believes that the people who have sought to take the lives of ourselves and every other Roman, who have endeavored to abolish the Republic and blot out its very name, should not for a single moment be permitted to live and enjoy the air we all breathe. . . . Caesar, on the other hand, takes the view that death has been appointed by the gods not as a punishment at all, but as an inevitable natural happening, or a relief from toil and trouble. . . . Whereas, imprisonment [for life], he says . . . was unmistakably devised as the special penalty for atrocious crimes. He moves, therefore, that the defendants should be imprisoned.

walks right into the Senate. He joins in our national debates—watches and notes and marks down with his gaze each one of us he plots to assassinate![39]

Not surprisingly, Catiline fled Rome, and he and most of his followers were soon defeated and killed by Antonius in a small pitched battle. Meanwhile, under the authority of the senatorial last decree, soldiers rounded up those conspirators who had remained in the city. The main focus of the drama then shifted to the Senate House once again. In the heat of the moment, Cicero and several senators advocated that the conspirators be executed immediately, without benefit of a trial. This was a clear violation of Roman law, which allowed all people accused of a crime the right of trial before sentencing.

At this point, Julius Caesar, then a young politician seeking to enhance his already growing public image, asked to be allowed to speak. (He was already a member of the Senate because he had earlier served as quaestor and aedile.) He wisely foresaw that Cicero's ultra-patriotic zeal might later backfire on him and made sure to place himself on the legally correct side of the debate. "You must take care that the [conspirators'] guilt does not outweigh your sense of what is fitting," Caesar told his fellow senators,

and that you do not indulge your resentment at the expense of your reputation. If a punishment can be found that is really adequate to their crimes, I am willing to support a departure from precedent; but if the enormity of their wickedness is such that no one could devise a fitting penalty, then I think we should content ourselves with those provided by the laws. . . . You, gentlemen, must consider the precedent that you establish for others. All bad precedents originate from measures good in themselves. [But] when power passes into the hands of ignorant or unworthy men, the precedent which you establish by inflicting an extraordinary penalty on guilty men who deserve it will be used against innocent men who do not deserve it.[40]

Caesar went on to recommend an alternative punishment—that the conspirators be imprisoned and their belongings confiscated. Moreover, he warned that people tend to remember best those events that have happened most recently; thus, well after the conspirators' deeds faded in significance, the Roman people would remember only the senators' rash and harsh judgment and departure from the law.

This prediction turned out to be accurate. Cicero and the others ignored

Caesar's plea, executed the prisoners, and enjoyed momentary popularity as great patriots. However, in time public opinion turned against the Senate for its abuse of established law and tradition. And for his opposition and effort to stop that abuse, Caesar looked like a wise and courageous leader, an image he later shrewdly exploited. In this way, the Senate's misuse of one of its most potent powers became a factor in the decline of that body. At the time, no one could have foreseen that the end of the Republic and senatorial predominance in Roman affairs was only a few years away.

CHAPTER 5

POLITICAL AND SOCIAL INFLUENCE OF SENATORS

Much has been said about the entrenched and formidable political authority and powers possessed by senators during most of Rome's republican years. It has also been established that Roman senators exercised an enormous amount of influence in various areas of Roman society. Far less has been said about exactly how these men maintained their authority and influence over the rest of their countrymen. It is not enough to say that senators wielded great prestige and authority simply because they were rich, came from noble families, or were the guardians of ancient tradition. All of these statements are true and affected how the senators performed their duties. Yet these are only the more obvious surface characteristics of the time-honored office they held. Their work in that office was also affected by, and indeed could not have been accomplished at all without, a great deal of political and social custom and maneuvering, much of which existed beneath the outward surface of government.

One way the senators wielded their disproportionate influence was through subtle manipulation of the citizen assemblies. Another was through a social system in which the senators took advantage of favors owed them by ordinary citizens. Still another way senators maintained their influence was by resisting changes in the political and social status quo. In the last century of the Republic, a growing minority of senators attempted to achieve their aims by allying themselves with the tribunes and people against the majority of conservative senators. This factional infighting within the Senate was one of the factors that weakened that body and brought about the end of the Republic.

MANIPULATION OF THE VOTERS

The reality was that most senators preferred to use the existing system to manipulate the plebeian voters rather than to form true political alliances with them. A prime example is the way senators could and often did influence the voting in the Centuriate assembly (*comitia centuriata*), the popular body that elected Rome's high magistrates and approved war declarations and peace treaties. This influence, which was largely indirect and covert, was possible because of the peculiar structure and voting procedures of the assembly. Modern Americans are used to the "one person–one vote" system. In the U.S. House of Representatives, the state legislatures, and town meetings on the local level, each member has the right to cast his or her individual vote.

In Rome's Centuriate assembly, by contrast, the people voted in groups, or blocs, rather than individually. Each bloc was called a century, the term from which the name of the body came. There were 193 centuries in all, each of which had an equal voice in any vote. The most important factor determining which century a person belonged to was the value of his property—basically his net worth. So some centuries were made up strictly of poor people and others of well-to-do people. Because there were a great deal more poor people than rich people, the poor had much larger centuries than the rich.

At first glance, it might seem that having larger voting blocs would give poorer voters an advantage. However, each century had only one vote, regardless of how many members it had. The most crucial factor, and the one the senators regularly took advantage of, was the order of the voting. The smaller centuries, which were filled with men closely connected to the patrician senators, always voted first. When a majority of centuries was reached, the voting stopped; so some of the larger centuries, containing mainly less-well-off commoners, frequently did not get a chance to vote. Thus, if the senators wanted the voting in the assembly to go a certain way, they instructed their associates in the wealthier centuries to vote accordingly.

THE MORNING SALUTE

But what factors made these members of the assembly "associates" of the senators? Why would free Roman men almost always vote as the senators desired rather than follow the dictates of their conscience and personal opinions? The answer lies in one of the most important and influential of all Roman social institutions—patronage. This system, in which the heads of well-to-do families became the patrons (*patroni*) of less-well-off clients (*clientes*), was deeply ingrained in Roman society. It originated in the dim past, perhaps in the early Monarchy, as suggested in this passage by Dionysius of Halicarnassus about the Roman founder:

> Romulus entrusted the plebeians to the protection of the patricians, but permitted each plebeian to choose for his patron whom he himself wished. This system is called patronage. Romulus then established these rules about patronage. It was the duty of the patricians to explain the laws to their clients [partly because the clients were illiterate and uneducated], to bring suits on their behalf if they were wronged or injured, and to defend them against prosecutors. . . . It was unlawful and unholy for patricians and clients to bring suit against one another, to testify against one another in court, or to vote against the other.[41]

In spite of ancient passages like this one, it is difficult, if not impossible, to

ꙅ RULES OF ETIQUETTE ꙮ
FOR POLITE PATRONS

Not all high-placed Roman patrons were the haughty, rude types mentioned by Seneca the Younger. As Quintus Cicero makes clear in a letter to his famous brother (translated here by Jo-Ann Shelton in her sourcebook on Roman social history), the Ciceros and men like them treated their clients more politely.

The morning greeters are more common than the other two groups and more numerous, because this is now the fashion. You must be sure to make the slightest little service they do seem especially gratifying to you. Indicate to those who come to your house that you are aware of their attention. Make it known to their friends (who will, of course, report your words to them). And tell them often, in person. When several candidates are campaigning and men see that there is one who really appreciates the services of his attendants, they frequently desert the other candidates and pledge themselves to him. . . . As for the group who escort you from your home, whose service is greater than that of the morning greeters, clearly indicate to them that it is also more gratifying to you. . . . Now the third group in this classification are those who attend you assiduously [constantly and faithfully]. Some do voluntarily; make sure that they know that you will be under obligation to them for this enormous favor.

know exactly when these rules of patronage were instituted. The notion that a single ruler, in this case Romulus, created them was probably a convenient assumption made by Dionysius, Livy, and other writers of late republican times. It is more likely that patronage, including the leading role senators played in it, developed gradually over the course of Rome's first few centuries. What is more certain is that in the mid- to late Republic

ও FROM PATRON TO GODFATHER ৬

In her useful book As the Romans Did, *noted University of California scholar Jo-Ann Shelton provides some basic facts about the Roman patronage system, which, she points out, was so ingrained that parts of it survived Rome's fall.*

The patronage system was one of the most deep-rooted and pervasive aspects of ancient Roman society. It has endured into modern Italian society where a *padrone*, or "godfather," offers protection and assistance to those less wealthy and powerful than himself, and in turn acquires a "clientele" of loyal supporters. . . . By the middle of the republican period, not only patricians were patrons. As some plebeian families gained power and wealth, they were in a position to become patrons. Most patrons were of senatorial rank and devoted their lives to the advancement of their own political careers. . . . The patronage system had originated as a relationship between free citizens.

However, slaves who were given their freedom became clients of their former owners, who became their patrons.

A group of clients accompanies an elderly patron to a public event, a show of support that enhanced his prestige.

(roughly the third to first century B.C.) a patrician patron's dependent plebeian clients usually voted as he directed and supported him in other ways in exchange for his financial and legal protection. In addition, freed slaves were expected to become the clients of their former masters.

One way that plebeian clients showed respect and subservience to senators and other high-placed patrons was through the *salutatio*, or "morning salute." It consisted of a group of clients paying a morning visit to their patron's home. There he would greet them and, if he was gracious and polite enough, ask how they and their families were doing. Often he would then send them on errands or assign them tasks to fulfill; these were viewed as part of their payback for the favors they owed him. At times a patron bestowed small gifts on one or more of his clients or invited them to dinner. (Most clients greatly appreciated the chance to attend such functions, where they might meet and make an impression on people with money and influence.)

If the senator or other patron had no errands to assign during the morning salute, he might simply give his clients a nod and go about his business. Sometimes a patron would not even bother with a nod. In a passage from one of his surviving essays, the Roman playwright Seneca the Younger describes the rude behavior exhibited by some of the more arrogant and insensitive upper-class patrons:

How many [patrons] will deny [their clients] admittance because they are asleep, or disinclined for activity, or merely rude? How many, after tormenting them with long waiting, will dash by on a pretense of urgent business! How many will avoid going out through the reception hall which is crowded with callers and escape through a . . . back door? . . . How many, still groggy . . . from the last night's debauch [drinking party], will yawn offensively to a man who has broken his own sleep to wait upon another's finishing his and mumble a greeting through half-open lips?[42]

STRATEGIES TO WIN OVER THE COMMON PEOPLE

However a senator behaved during the *salutatio*, he typically expected a great deal from his clients. A client not only supported his patron at election time but also attended court sessions, dinners and banquets, poetry readings, or any other gatherings where the patron's prestige might be enhanced by the show of a loyal following. A poor or middle-class client might be expected to accompany the patron on some social or business calls, for example. Afterward, the client might be rewarded with a small amount of money or the much coveted dinner invitation. A fairly detailed description of the political and other favors patrons expected and received from their clients has survived; it appears in a passage from a long letter written to the great senator Marcus Tullius Cicero by his brother, Quintus, a noted soldier and political administrator. "Make sure that you are attended every day by men from each class, order, and age group," the passage begins.

> Your attendants can also be divided into three groups: (1) those who come to your home for the morning salutation, (2) those who escort you from your home [to the Senate House, Forum, law court, or elsewhere], and (3) those who follow you through the city [as you go about your daily routine]. The morning greeters are more common than the other two groups and more numerous, because this is now the fashion. . . . [However, the service provided by] the group who escort you from your home . . . is greater than that of the morning greeters. . . . Come down to the Forum at the same time every day; for a large crowd of escorts every day brings you great renown and great respect. Now the third group in this classification are those who attend you assiduously [constant-

ly and faithfully]. Some do voluntarily; make sure that they know that you will be under obligation to them for this enormous favor. Some, however, owe you this service. Simply demand that they repay you. Those whose age and occupation will allow it should attend you constantly, but those who cannot personally attend you should assign their relatives to this duty.[43]

Having established the duties of clients to leading Romans, including senators, Quintus Cicero listed the steps a politician like his brother should take "to win over the common people." He emphasizes that "you need flattery, constant attention, courtesy, good reputation . . . and [whenever possible] the knowledge of each man's name." In fact, he says, a government official should practice memorizing names "so that every day you become even better at this." The younger Cicero adds that one should "make it clear" to the people "that you will do whatever you do [in the capacity of your office] with enthusiasm and generosity."[44] It appears that much of the advice given by Quintus Cicero in the letter pertained directly to his brother's campaign for the consulship of 63 B.C., but the points made about the exploitation of clients and voters by the well-to-do and powerful applied just as well to Cicero's position as a

Julius Caesar (at right) used his wealth and family prestige to acquire fame and power. He became a senator, general, and ultimately dictator.

senator. During Rome's republican years, senators benefited from the patronage system more than any others in society.

In these ways, therefore, a majority of ordinary Roman voters were beholden in some way to either senators or well-to-do men who were friends of senators or strong supporters of the Senate and its policies. In addition to the obvious ways in which this state of affairs perpetuated the authority and prestige of the senators, it significantly diminished the independence and ultimate authority of the assembly. And this kept Rome from becoming a true democracy like Athens and a number of other Greek states that were contemporary with the Republic. Michael Grant explains:

> Here was another reason why [Rome's popular] assembly, for all its impressive democratic-sounding "powers," could never be a truly democratic body. . . . Not only were its richest members in possession of disproportionate voting power, but those assemblymen who lacked wealth were, for the most part, clients of rich men and senators in whose favor . . . they were duty bound to cast their votes in the annual elections to state offices. On the credit side, it might be said that a poor client's relationship to his patron, based on inescapable ties of good faith, gave his life meaning and security that poor people in other countries have frequently lacked and still lack today. Nevertheless, [the institution of patronage] acted as a powerful brake on democratic development and indeed helped to prevent it from ever taking place.[45]

INFLUENCE WIELDED BY SENATORIAL "PARTIES"

The antidemocratic bias of most senators and the actions they took to maintain the supremacy of the patrician and senatorial class were demonstrated clearly in the final century of

the Republic. In this period, the Senate saw its traditional authority steadily eroding under assaults from various quarters. In particular, a number of military generals and other powerful men, including Julius Caesar, increasingly used their own great wealth and influence to challenge the power of the Senate. Some of these men or their supporters were senators themselves. So a rift began to form in the senatorial ranks, and each of the opposing sides used its considerable influence in an attempt to overshadow the other. Sallust later summed up the motives and tactics of the power struggle:

> The nobles started to use their position, and the people their liberty, to gratify their selfish passions, every man snatching and seizing what he could for himself. So the whole community was split into parties. . . . The nobility [here meaning the conservatives in the senatorial class] had the advantage of being a close-knit body, whereas the democratic party [here referring to those senators and other high officials who sought the backing of the common people in the struggle] was weakened by its loose organization. . . . The possession of power [by these two groups] gave unlimited scope to ruthless greed, which violated and plundered everything.[46]

Despite Sallust's use of the term *parties*, Rome did not have formal political parties like those familiar in modern democracies such as the United States and Britain, with conventions, platforms, nominees, and so forth. The so-called parties of the late Republic were more informal, loosely organized factions whose goals, membership, and methods changed with the times. Cicero called the more conservative senators and their supporters the *optimates* (or *boni*, meaning "good men"), of which he was one. He called the members of the opposing group the *populares* because of their support among the popular masses.

The struggle between the *optimates* and *populares*, along with other factors, eventually doomed the senatorial profession (if it can be called such). It eventually came down to a case of the winds of change overcoming entrenched tradition, a common theme in history. Lily Ross Taylor, an expert on ancient Roman politics, explains that, in these crucial years,

the Senate was controlled by powerful nobles who were determined to uphold or regain the constitution of their ancestors and to keep for themselves and their associates the great gains of empire. . . . The opposition [was made up of tribunes] . . . and men belonging, as many of the tribunes

Though an aristocrat by birth, Julius Caesar shrewdly supported the populares *to further his goals.*

❧ MURDER IN THE SENATE ❧

The growing struggles between the old senatorial order and the military strongmen who challenged that order are most clearly seen in the series of power grabs made by Julius Caesar between 49 and 44 B.C. Eventually, he declared himself dictator for life. Most senators were appalled, and some hatched the most famous assassination plot in history. This account of Caesar's murder in the Senate House is by the Roman historian Suetonius (from his Lives of the Twelve Caesars*).*

As soon as Caesar took his seat, the conspirators crowded around him as if to pay their respects. Tillius Cimber . . . came up close, pretending to ask a question. Caesar made a gesture of postponement, but Cimber caught hold of his shoulders. "This is violence!" Caesar cried, and . . . as he turned away, one of the Casca brothers with a sweep of his dagger stabbed him just below the throat. . . . Twenty-three dagger thrusts went home as he stood there. Caesar did not utter a sound after Casca's blow had drawn a groan from him; though some say that when he saw Marcus Brutus about to deliver the second blow, he reproached him in Greek with: "You, too, my child?" [There were rumors that Brutus was Caesar's illegitimate son.] The entire Senate then dispersed in confusion, and Caesar was left lying dead for some time until three slave boys carried him home in a litter [stretcher], with one arm hanging over the side.

After killing Caesar (whose body lies at the base of Pompey's statue), the senators dash outside proclaiming "Liberty!"

did, to *optimate* families, who, having failed to gain their ends from the Senate, used tribunes to obtain from the popular assembly their special designs for armies and military commands.[47]

These armies and military commands proved to be the keys to ultimate power. *Populares* like Caesar gained armies that were more loyal to themselves than to the Senate, which was still largely controlled by old-fashioned stalwarts like Cicero. The ultimate result was a series of devastating civil wars that the conservatives lost. From the late first century B.C. on, Rome was ruled by Caesar's political heirs—the emperors—not by the Senate.

A MEASURE OF EXCELLENCE

These, then, are some of the ways the senators used and misused their high positions and great influence in Roman politics and society. The misuse got them into trouble and helped to bring about their loss of power. Still, viewed over the long time span of the Republic, it would not be an exaggeration to say that most senators, with all their human faults, did more good than harm for the Roman nation. As the late, great historian Will Durant puts it:

The Senate of the Republic often abused its authority, defended corrupt officials, waged war ruthlessly, exploited conquered provinces greedily, and suppressed the aspirations of the people for a larger share in the prosperity of Rome. But never elsewhere (except during the extraordinarily productive reigns of the "good emperors" in the second century A.D.) have so much energy, wisdom, and skill been applied to statesmanship. And never elsewhere has the idea of service to the state so dominated a government or a people. These senators were not supermen; they made serious mistakes, sometimes vacillated [wavered] in their policies, often lost the vision of empire in the lust for personal gain. But most of them had been magistrates, administrators, and commanders; some of them . . . had ruled provinces as large as kingdoms; many of them came of families that had given statesmen or generals to Rome for hundreds of years. It was impossible that a body made up of such men should escape some measure of excellence.[48]

THE SENATE DURING THE EMPIRE

The Roman Senate survived the collapse of the Republic, and senators continued to meet on a regular basis right up to and beyond the traditional date of the Empire's fall—A.D. 476. (This was the year that the last official Roman emperor, Romulus Augustulus, was deposed by German troops. The city of Rome and its institutions, including the Senate, remained intact for two more generations under Germanic rule.) Yet during the Empire, the senators no longer wielded the far-reaching powers they had in republican times. Their meetings and decrees became mainly ceremonial in nature, and their authority in most state affairs was a pale shadow of what it had once been.

THE FALL OF THE REPUBLIC

The Senate lost its supreme authority over much of Rome's governmental apparatus during the course of two tumultuous generations in the first century B.C. A series of ambitious, powerful military and political figures—among them Sulla, Pompey, Crassus, Caesar, Antony, and Octavian—ran roughshod over the traditional republican institutions. They amassed personal armies with which to intimidate their opponents, which often included the Senate, as well as one another.

To their credit, the senators did not go down without a fight. As one civil war after another rocked the Roman realm, old-style conservative senators mightily resisted and tried to salvage the dignity and authority of the Senate. In 44 B.C., a group of them, led by Marcus Brutus and Gaius Cassius, took action against Julius Caesar, who had declared himself dictator for life. They stabbed him to death in the Senate House, believing that they were restoring the faltering Senate and Republic.

But this was a delusion born of frustration and desperation. New strongmen, notably Caesar's hard-drinking lieutenant, Mark Antony, and Caesar's adopted son, Octavian, immediately filled the vacuum left by the dictator's demise. The great Cicero tried to meet these new threats. When Antony tried to assume some of Caesar's dictatorial powers, for example, the senator retaliated with a series of forceful speeches. "When I was a young man I defended our state," Cicero said.

In my old age I shall not abandon it. Having scorned the swords of Catiline, I shall not be intimidated by yours. On the contrary, I would gladly offer my own body, if my death could redeem the freedom of our nation.[49]

These turned out to be fateful and prophetic words for Cicero, the Senate, and the Republic alike. Antony and Octavian soon formed an alliance and murdered many senators, including

Antony's henchmen murder Cicero, Rome's last great republican champion. Shortly after Cicero's death, the Republic met its own demise.

Cicero. Then they defeated Brutus, Cassius, and the last remnants of senatorial resistance at Philippi, in Greece. As the power struggle continued, Antony and Octavian turned on each other. And still another civil war ensued, leaving Antony dead and Octavian in complete control of the Roman realm.

AUGUSTUS REMOLDS THE SENATE

The total victory of Octavian in 31–30 B.C. marked the final demise of the Republic and the beginning of a new era for the senators and their august body. Rome's new leader wisely refrained from calling himself dictator (although in fact he was), as Caesar had. Indeed, Octavian called himself only *princeps*, meaning "first citizen," and made a point of maintaining the offices and institutions of the Republic, including the consuls and Senate. Though these were now mere trappings, with almost no real powers, keeping them gave the people the comfort of tradition and the illusion of representative government.

Meanwhile, the now near-powerless senators had no choice but to support Octavian's transformation of the dead Republic into what became known as the Roman Empire. In 27 B.C., they bestowed on him the title of Augustus, the "revered one." And though he never called himself an emperor, he was in fact the first of a

long line of imperial rulers. "Through this process," the second-century Romanized Greek historian Dio Cassius writes,

the power both of the people and of the Senate was wholly transferred into the hands of Augustus, and it was from this time that a monarchy, strictly speaking, was established. It would certainly be the most truthful to describe it as a monarchy. . . . The Senate as a whole continued to sit . . . as it had done before . . . but nothing was done without Augustus's approval.[50]

Under Augustus and his heirs, the senators still enjoyed considerable prestige and moral authority, even if their powers were limited. Among these powers was control over the administration of some of the provinces. According to Dio, Augustus

handed over the weaker provinces to the Senate . . . but kept the stronger under his authority. . . . The real object of this arrangement was that the senators should be unarmed and unprepared for war, while he possessed arms and controlled the troops.[51]

Under the emperors the Senate also continued to maintain the state treasury, at least on paper. In reality, the senators no longer wielded the actual powers of the purse, as the emperor could overrule them and spend as much as he wanted on whatever he liked. In addition, senators conducted high-profile trials, especially those involving treason, during the Empire. And after popular elections were discontinued in the early first century A.D., the senators took over the job of electing the magistrates who administered the state on a daily basis. These elections were fixed, however. The emperor selected the candidates he desired to see serve and the senators duly rubber-stamped them into office.

A NEW SENATE IN THE EAST

Even in its new servile form, the Senate remained a symbol of Roman tradition, and membership ensured a man an honored place in society. In fact, the Senate had become so ingrained an institution that no emperor dared abolish it (though several wanted to). Accordingly, when the emperor

This drawing is based on a statue of Augustus, the first emperor, found at Prima Porta, near Rome. During the Empire, the Senate had few real powers.

Constantine I inaugurated the city of Constantinople as the Empire's eastern capital in the 330s A.D., he set up an eastern version of the Senate. Within a few years, the eastern Senate was as large and prestigious as the western one back in Rome.

In the end, the eastern Roman Senate outlived the western one. In the late 500s A.D., the German rulers of Rome could not hold what little was left of the old imperial lands together. In the wake of new invasions of tribal peoples from the north, Rome and other Italian cities were largely depopulated and the Senate finally ceased to exist. The eastern Senate survived and remained a prestigious body within the surviving portion of the Roman realm, which steadily morphed into the Byzantine Empire. Like the defunct western imperial Roman Senate, the Byzantine version usually did little more than rubber-stamp the policies of the emperors. The last official meetings of the Byzantine Senate took place in 1453, the year the Ottoman Turks captured Constantinople and wiped out the last remaining vestiges of ancient Rome.

Yet all was not lost. At that fateful historical moment, almost exactly fifteen centuries had passed since the death of the indomitable Cicero. In his writings and those of some of his contemporaries, the voices and spirit of a long line of venerable republican senators still lived. And as long as people can read and remember, they will never be stilled.

INTRODUCTION:
POWER AND PRESTIGE: THE ORIGINS OF THE ROMAN SENATE

1. Livy, *The History of Rome from Its Foundation*, books 1–5 published as *Livy: The Early History of Rome*, trans. Aubrey de Sélincourt. New York: Penguin, 1960, pp. 42–43.
2. Polybius, *The Histories*, published as *Polybius: The Rise of the Roman Empire*, trans. Ian Scott-Kilvert. New York: Penguin, 1979, pp. 313–14.
3. T.J. Cornell, *The Beginnings of Rome: Italy and Rome from the Bronze Age to the Punic Wars (c.1000–264 B.C.)*. London: Routledge, 1995, p. 248.
4. Cornell, *Beginnings of Rome*, p. 370.

CHAPTER 1:
BECOMING A ROMAN SENATOR

5. Polybius, *Histories*, p. 312.
6. Polybius, *Histories*, p. 317.
7. Cicero, *Laws*, in *Cicero: On Government*, trans. Michael Grant. New York: Penguin, 1993, p. 196.
8. Livy, *Early History of Rome*, p. 141.
9. Livy, *Early History of Rome*, p. 142.
10. Robert C. Byrd, *The Senate of the Roman Republic: Addresses on the History of Roman Constitutional-

ism*. Washington, DC: U.S. Government Printing Office, 1994, p. 32.
11. Cicero, *De Officiis (On Duties)*, trans. Walter Miller. Cambridge, MA: Harvard University Press, 1961, pp. 57–58.
12. Keith Hopkins, *Conquerors and Slaves: Sociological Studies in Roman History*, vol. 1. New York: Cambridge University Press, 1978, p. 124.
13. Cicero, *On Duties*, pp. 36–37.

CHAPTER 2:
DOMESTIC POWERS OF SENATORS

14. Polybius, *Histories*, p. 316.
15. Polybius, *Histories*, p. 316.
16. Polybius, *Histories*, p. 313.
17. Polybius, *Histories*, pp. 316–17.
18. Plutarch, *Life of Tiberius Gracchus*, in *Makers of Rome: Nine Lives by Plutarch*, trans. Ian Scott-Kilvert. New York: Penguin, 1965, p. 163.
19. F.R. Cowell, *Cicero and the Roman Republic*. Baltimore, MD: Penguin, 1967, p. 138.
20. Livy, *The History of Rome from Its Foundation*, books 21–30 published as *Livy: The War with Hannibal*, trans. Aubrey de Sélincourt. New York: Penguin, 1972, p. 102.
21. Livy, *War with Hannibal*, p. 103.
22. Plutarch, *Life of Crassus*, in *Fall of*

the Roman Republic: Six Lives by Plutarch, trans. Rex Warner. New York: Penguin, 1972, p. 124.

23. Plutarch, *Crassus*, in *Fall of the Roman Republic*, p. 126.

CHAPTER 3: THE SENATE AND FOREIGN RELATIONS

24. Polybius, *Histories*, pp. 313–14.
25. Cowell, *Cicero and the Roman Republic*, p. 137.
26. Polybius, *Histories*, p. 192.
27. Livy, *War with Hannibal*, p. 29.
28. Polybius, *Histories*, p. 209.
29. Livy, *War with Hannibal*, pp. 671, 673.
30. Livy, *War with Hannibal*, pp. 673–74.
31. Polybius, *Histories*, pp. 480–81.
32. Polybius, *Histories*, pp. 481–82.
33. Livy, *The History of Rome from Its Foundation*, books 31–45 published as *Livy: Rome and the Mediterranean*, trans. Henry Bettenson. New York: Penguin, 1976, p. 611.
34. Plutarch, *Life of Cato*, in *Makers of Rome*, p. 149.

CHAPTER 4: SENATORIAL MEETINGS, SPEECHES, AND DECREES

35. Quoted in Anthony Everitt, *Cicero: The Life and Times of Rome's Greatest Politician*. New York: Random House, 2001, p. 29.
36. Byrd, *The Senate of the Roman Republic*, p. 44.
37. Quoted in Jo-Ann Shelton, ed., *As the Romans Did: A Sourcebook*

in Roman Social History. New York: Oxford University Press, 1988, p. 400.

38. Sallust, *The Conspiracy of Catiline*, in *Sallust: The Jugurthine War / The Conspiracy of Catiline*, trans. S.A. Handford. New York: Penguin, 1988, p. 196.
39. Cicero, *First Speech Against Catiline*, in *Selected Political Speeches of Cicero*, trans. Michael Grant. Baltimore, MD: Penguin, 1979, p. 76.
40. Quoted in Sallust, *Conspiracy of Catiline*, pp. 216–19.

CHAPTER 5: POLITICAL AND SOCIAL INFLUENCE OF SENATORS

41. Quoted in Shelton, *As the Romans Did*, p. 14.
42. Seneca the Younger, *On the Shortness of Life*, in Moses Hadas, trans. and ed., *The Stoic Philosophy of Seneca*. New York: W.W. Norton, 1958, p. 66.
43. Quoted in Shelton, *As the Romans Did*, pp. 222–23.
44. Quoted in Shelton, *As the Romans Did*, p. 223.
45. Michael Grant, *History of Rome*. New York: Scribner's, 1978, pp. 70–71.
46. Sallust, *The Jugurthine War*, in *Sallust: The Jugurthine War / The Conspiracy of Catiline*, pp. 77–78.
47. Lily Ross Taylor, *Party Politics in the Age of Caesar*. Berkeley and Los Angeles: University of California Press, 1968, p. 14.

48. Will Durant, *Caesar and Christ: A History of Roman Civilization and of Christianity from Their Beginnings to A.D. 325.* New York: Simon and Schuster, 1944, p. 28.

EPILOGUE:
THE SENATE DURING THE EMPIRE

49. Cicero, *Second Philippic,* in *Cicero: Selected Works,* trans. Michael Grant. New York: Penguin, 1984, p. 152.

50. Dio Cassius, *Roman History: The Reign of Augustus,* trans. Ian Scott-Kilvert. New York: Penguin, 1987, pp. 144–45.

51. Dio Cassius, *Roman History,* p. 135.

CHRONOLOGY

753 B.C.
Traditional date for Rome's founding by its legendary first king, Romulus.

509
Rome's leading citizens, the patrician senators, depose the kings and establish the Republic.

494
The so-called Conflict of the Orders, in which Rome's commoners demand to share power with the powerful men of the senatorial class, begins.

450
The commoners succeed in getting the laws governing society written down in the form of the Twelve Tables.

366
For the first time, commoners have the right to become consuls and senators.

ca. 339–332
The Lex Ovinia, which allows the censors to enroll men in the Senate, where they could serve for life, is passed.

234
Cato the Censor, who will become one of Rome's most influential senators, is born.

218
The Senate faces a supreme test of its domestic security authority when the Carthaginian general Hannibal crosses the Alps and invades Italy, during the Second Punic War.

201
Rome defeats Carthage and the Senate concludes the peace treaty.

186
Fearing a lapse of morality, the senators ban the rites of the religious cult of the fertility god Bacchus.

180
The *cursus honorum*, the traditional ladder of high public offices leading to entry into the Senate, is fixed by law.

153
On a senatorial mission, Cato visits Carthage and is disturbed to see it thriving once more.

149
Thanks in large part to Cato's insistence, the Romans launch the Third Punic War, which ends with Carthage's complete destruction.

74
Cicero, perhaps the greatest Roman senator of all, enters the Senate.

63
Cicero is instrumental in stopping a plot to seize control of the govern-

ment. At his urgings, the Senate executes the surviving ringleaders.

52
The Senate House is destroyed by fire.

49
The powerful military general Julius Caesar initiates a civil war in which he opposes the Senate and its authority.

44
After declaring himself dictator for life, Caesar is assassinated by a group of senators.

43
Cicero is murdered by his political enemies.

31–30
Octavian, Caesar's adopted son, wins the last of the civil wars and gains control of the entire Roman realm.

29
A new Senate House begun by Julius Caesar is completed.

27
The now nearly powerless senators give Octavian the title of Augustus, "the revered one."

A.D. 283
The Senate House burns down again. This time the emperor Diocletian rebuilds it, producing the version that survives today.

476
The last western Roman emperor is deposed.

FOR FURTHER READING

BOOKS

Fiona Forsyth, *Cicero: Defender of the Republic*. New York: Rosen, 2003. A well-written synopsis of the life and contributions of one of the greatest of all the Roman senators—Marcus Tullius Cicero.

Robert B. Kebric, *Roman People*. Mountain View, CA: Mayfield, 2001. This excellent volume by one of the leading scholars of ancient Rome contains a good deal of clearly stated information about ancient Roman government, including the Senate.

Don Nardo, *From Founding to Fall: A History of Rome*. San Diego: Lucent Books, 2003. A readable, useful general overview of Roman history, including Rome's changes in government.

Richard Platt, *Julius Caesar: Great Dictator of Rome*. London: Dorling Kindersley, 2001. An excellent introduction to one of the greatest Roman figures, who was often at odds with and successfully weakened the Senate.

Judith Simpson, *Ancient Rome*. New York: Time-Life Books, 1997. One of Time-Life's library of picture books about the ancient world, this one is beautifully illustrated with attractive and appropriate photographs and paintings. The general but well-written text is aimed at intermediate young readers.

INTERNET SOURCES

Discovery Channel, "Clients and Patrons." http://myron.sjsu.edu/rome web/SOCIAL/art2.htm. An excellent overview of the Roman institution of patronage, one of the main tools senators used to maintain their power.

History Net, "Curia: The House of the Roman Senate." http://ancient history.about.com/cs/romearchi tecture/a/aa012903a.htm. Provides general information about the Senate House and links to further research about ancient Rome.

Illustrated History of the Roman Empire, "Roman Dress." www.roman-empire.net/society/soc-dress.html. A very informative site about everyday Roman clothing, including the toga, which every senator wore, supplemented by photos and drawings.

Barbara F. McManus, "Roman *Cursus Honorum*." www.vroma.org/~bmc manus/romangvt.html. An excellent overview of the offices of the ancient Roman Republican government.

Skidmore College, "Anatomy of a Conspiracy." www.skidmore.edu/academics/classics/courses/1999spring/c1201/c1201pro/c1201see.html. Contains background information about and a year-by-year chronology of the main figures of the Catilinian conspiracy that rocked the Roman Senate in the first century B.C.

WORKS CONSULTED

MAJOR WORKS

Robert C. Byrd, *The Senate of the Roman Republic: Addresses on the History of Roman Constitutionalism.* Washington, DC: U.S. Government Printing Office, 1994. A masterful telling of the trials and tribulations of the Roman Republic, emphasizing the role of the Senate and its privileged members.

T.J. Cornell, *The Beginnings of Rome: Italy and Rome from the Bronze Age to the Punic Wars (c.1000–264 B.C.).* London: Routledge, 1995. A well-written, authoritative study of Rome's early centuries, including a great deal on Rome's early government and how the Senate came to be.

F.R. Cowell, *Cicero and the Roman Republic.* Baltimore, MD: Penguin, 1967. A very detailed and insightful analysis of the late Republic, its leaders, the Senate in decline, and the problems that caused the Republic to collapse.

Michael Crawford, *The Roman Republic.* Cambridge, MA: Harvard University Press, 1993. One of the best available overviews of the Republic, offering various insights into the nature of the political, cultural, and intellectual forces that shaped the decisions of Roman leaders.

Anthony Everitt, *Cicero: The Life and Times of Rome's Greatest Politician.* New York: Random House, 2001. A fine new telling of the deeds, works, and influence of one of republican Rome's greatest senators.

Michael Grant, *Caesar*, London: Weidenfeld and Nicolson, 1974. A fine telling of Caesar's exploits and importance by one of the most prolific classical historians.

———, *History of Rome.* New York: Scribner's, 1978. Comprehensive, insightful, and well written, this is one of the best available general overviews of Roman civilization from its founding to its fall.

Philip Matyszak, *Chronicle of the Roman Republic.* New York: Thames and Hudson, 2003. A useful overview of the Republic, with plenty of information about the leading figures and their interaction with the Senate.

R.J. Talbert, *The Senate of Imperial Rome.* Princeton, NJ: Princeton University Press, 1987. A well-written examination of the Senate and its key role in Roman government.

OTHER IMPORTANT WORKS

PRIMARY SOURCES

Appian, *Roman History.* Trans, Horace White. Cambridge, MA: Harvard University Press, 1964; and excerpted in *Appian: The Civil Wars.* Trans. John Carter. New York: Penguin, 1996.

Cicero, *De Officiis (On Duties).* Trans. Walter Miller. Cambridge, MA: Harvard University Press, 1961; *Cicero: Murder Trials.* Trans. Michael Grant. New York: Penguin, 1990; *Cicero: On Government.* Trans. Michael Grant. New York: Penguin, 1993; *Cicero: Selected Works.* Trans. Michael Grant. New York: Penguin, 1984; *Letters to Atticus.* Trans. D.R. Shackleton Bailey. 4 vols. Cambridge, MA: Harvard University Press, 1999; *Letters to Friends.* Trans. D.R. Shackleton Bailey. 3 vols. Cambridge, MA: Harvard University Press, 2001; *The Republic* and *The Laws.* Trans. Niall Rudd. New York: Oxford University Press, 1998; and *Selected Political Speeches of Cicero.* Trans. Michael Grant. Baltimore, MD: Penguin, 1979.

Dio Cassius, *Roman History: The Reign of Augustus.* Trans. Ian Scott-Kilvert. New York: Penguin, 1987.

Dionysius of Halicarnassus, *Roman Antiquities.* Trans. Ernest Cary. 7 vols. Cambridge, MA: Harvard University Press, 1963.

Livy, *The History of Rome from Its Foundation*, books 1–5 published as *Livy: The Early History of Rome.* Trans. Aubrey de Sélincourt. New York: Penguin, 1960; books 6–10 published as *Livy: Rome and Italy.* Trans. Betty Radice. New York: Penguin, 1982; books 21–30 published as *Livy: The War with Hannibal.* Trans. Aubrey de Sélincourt. New York: Penguin, 1972; books 31–45 published as *Livy: Rome and the Mediterranean.* Trans. Henry Bettenson. New York: Penguin, 1976. Also, various books excerpted in *Livy.* Vol. 2. Trans. Canon Roberts. New York: E.P. Dutton, 1912.

Plutarch, *Parallel Lives*, published complete as *Lives of the Noble Grecians and Romans.* Trans. John Dryden. New York: Random House, 1932; also excerpted in *Fall of the Roman Republic: Six Lives by Plutarch.* Trans. Rex Warner. New York: Penguin, 1972; and *Makers of Rome: Nine Lives by Plutarch.* Trans. Ian Scott-Kilvert. New York: Penguin, 1965.

Polybius, *The Histories*, published as *Polybius: The Rise of the Roman Empire.* Trans. Ian Scott-Kilvert. New York: Penguin, 1979.

Sallust, *Works.* Trans. J.C. Rolfe. Cambridge, England: Cambridge University Press, 1965; also, *Sallust: The Jugurthine War / The Conspiracy of Catiline.* Trans. S.A. Handford. New York: Penguin, 1988.

Seneca the Younger, selected works in Moses Hadas, trans, and ed., *The Stoic Philosophy of Seneca.* New York: W.W. Norton, 1958.

Jo-Ann Shelton, ed., *As the Romans Did: A Sourcebook in Roman Social History.* New York: Oxford University Press, 1988.

Suetonius, *Lives of the Twelve Caesars,* published as *The Twelve Caesars.* Trans. Robert Graves. Rev. Michael Grant. New York: Penguin, 1979.

MODERN SOURCES

Lesley Adkins and Roy A. Adkins, *Handbook to Life in Ancient Rome.* New York: Facts On File, 1994.

E. Badian, *Roman Imperialism in the Late Republic.* Ithaca, NY: Cornell University Press, 1968.

Arthur E.R. Boak and William G. Sinnigen, *A History of Rome to 565 A.D.* New York: Macmillan, 1965.

Brian Caven, *The Punic Wars.* New York: Barnes and Noble, 1992.

Will Durant, *Caesar and Christ: A History of Roman Civilization and of Christianity from Their Beginnings to A.D. 325.* New York: Simon and Schuster, 1944.

Charles Freeman, *The World of the Romans.* New York: Oxford University Press, 1993.

Erich S. Gruen, *Culture and National Identity in Republican Rome.* Ithaca, NY: Cornell University Press, 1995.

———, *The Last Generation of the Roman Republic.* Berkeley and Los Angeles: University of California Press, 1974.

Christian Habicht, *Cicero the Politician.* Baltimore, MD: Johns Hopkins University Press, 1990.

Keith Hopkins, *Conquerors and Slaves: Sociological Studies in Roman History.* Vol. 1. New York: Cambridge University Press, 1978.

Ramon L. Jimenez, *Caesar Against Rome: The Great Roman Civil War.* London: Praeger, 2000.

Thomas N. Mitchell, *Cicero: The Senior Statesman.* New Haven, CT: Yale University Press, 1991.

Friedrich Munzer, *Roman Aristocratic Parties and Families.* Trans. Therese Ridley. Baltimore, MD: Johns Hopkins University Press, 1999.

Henry T. Rowell, *Rome in the Augustan Age.* Norman: University of Oklahoma Press, 1962.

Chris Scarre, *Chronicle of the Roman Emperors.* New York: Thames and Hudson, 1995.

H.H. Scullard, *Roman Politics, 220–150 B.C.* Oxford, England: Clarendon Press, 1973.

Ronald Syme, *The Roman Revolution.* New York: Oxford University Press, 1960.

Lily Ross Taylor, *Party Politics in the Age of Caesar.* Berkeley and Los Angeles: University of California Press, 1968.

PICTURE CREDITS

ABOUT THE AUTHOR

Classical historian Don Nardo has published many volumes about ancient Roman history and culture, including *The Punic Wars*, *The Age of Augustus*, *A Travel Guide to Ancient Rome*, *Life of a Roman Gladiator*, *Greek and Roman Science*, and Greenhaven Press's massive *Encyclopedia of Greek and Roman Mythology*. Mr. Nardo also writes screenplays and teleplays and composes music. He lives in Massachusetts with his wife, Christine.